Sweetness

Sweetness

DELICIOUS BAKED TREATS FOR EVERY OCCASION

Sarah Levy

S
SURREY BOOKS

CHICAGO

Printed in Malaysia.

Design by Brandtner Design.

Library of Congress Cataloging-in-Publication Data

Levy, Sarah, 1981-
Sweetness : delicious baked treats for every occasion / Sarah Levy.
     p. cm.
Includes index.
Summary: "A guide for the amateur cook to making sweets, treats, and confections for
special occasions"--Provided by publisher.
ISBN-13: 978-1-57284-093-5 (hardcover)
ISBN-10: 1-57284-093-5 (hardcover)
1. Desserts. 2. Baking. I. Title.
TX773.L468 2009
641.8'6--dc22
                                              2009011931

09 10 12 13   10 9 8 7 6 5 4 3 2 1

Surrey Books is an imprint of Agate Publishing. Agate books are available in bulk
at discount prices. For more information, go to agatepublishing.com.

To my mom and dad, for passing along a passion for food and for giving me the freedom and support to pursue my dreams.

Table of Contents

Introduction   9

Part One: What It Takes to Make Delicious and Beautiful Treats   13

    My Story   14

    My Secrets   17

Part Two: The Recipes   35

    Work   36

    Social Gatherings   50

    Matters of Love   68

    Day-to-Day Happenings   84

    Hostess Gifts   102

    Holidays   118

Acknowledgments   134

About the Author   137

Index   138

Introduction

I REALIZED AT A YOUNG AGE that there was no quicker route to happiness than through good food. Food has the ability to make me, as well as those around me, happy. Since opening my own bakery in 2004, I've witnessed how the right freshly baked treat can transform a date, TV night with the girls, or just another day at work into a special occasion. You can brighten someone's day with a chocolate-covered strawberry, or wiggle your way out of a predicament with a well-placed cookie.

As a busy city girl myself, I know firsthand how hard it can be to balance the demands of work, family, and social life. You can think of this book as a good way to cut to the chase and make beautiful and delicious treats even on a hectic schedule. I've simplified the recipes, and I've added charts that list the major ingredients and tools used in the book (see pages 30–33), so you can quickly figure out what you have on hand and what you need to buy.

Sometimes it's hard to figure out what to make for a certain occasion. *Sweetness* is a guide to help you make the right choice every time.

- Wondering how to impress your boyfriend's parents?

- Looking for a way to avoid hunger pangs on your next airplane trip?

- Stressed out about what to bring to that baby shower, wedding party, or holiday dinner?

All the answers are here. With the right portable treat, even your dreariest days will have a silver lining!

....

A QUICK NOTE ABOUT RECIPE DIFFICULTY

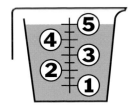

Next to each recipe's title, you'll see a little measuring cup. The measuring cup's fill line (which ranges from 1 to 5 cups) indicates the recipe's difficulty. A 5 is a real challenge (my Chocolate–Raspberry Brioche on page 130 jumps to mind), and a 1 is a great recipe for someone just getting started with baking and looking for a delicious, fast, and simple treat (check out my Grandma Eadie's Double Chocolate Chip Cake on page 44).

AND NOW, THE PLAYERS ...

This book contains a few recipes that were contributed by some of my favorite family members, friends, mentors, and coworkers. I would like to thank the people who have contributed recipes to *Sweetness* and to give you a little background information on each of them. Without the following people's contributions, this book would not have been possible.

Rafael Ornelas. Rafael is the head chef at Sarah's Pastries & Candies, and he was one of the reasons that I decided to open a pastry shop. Rafael was one of my very first bosses—I worked for him when I was only 19 years old—and over the years, he has taught me so many useful techniques (and life lessons). Rafael has always emphasized the importance of working fast and clean and of being able to multitask. His passion for pastry is contagious, and he's always dreaming up something new, tasty, and creative in the kitchen. Rafael has been with Sarah's Pastries & Candies since its inception in 2004, and I hope to be able to work with him forever. Although he's technically no longer my boss, I'll always look up to him. I turn to Rafael for advice on anything and everything regarding pastry! Rafael contributed the following recipes: Rafael's Righteous Cream-Cheese Brownies (page 41), Rafael's Pistachio Buttercream Filling (page 96), Rafael's Toffee Sugar Cookies (page 108), and Rafael's Coconut–Apricot Macaroons (page 121).

Mom (also known as Terry Levy). My mom, who happens to be the sweetest, most loving person in the world, holds the official title at Sarah's Pastries & Candies of "quality-control officer"—and believe me, that's a sought-after position! She was not the kind of mom who was always in the kitchen baking up something wonderful, but Mom has her own go-to dishes that she executes perfectly each and every time. She contributed the recipes for Mom's Fudge Brownie Sundaes (page 71), Mom's Almond Moon Cookies (page 39), and Mom's Granola (page 90)—but she'll tell you that the almond moon cookie and brownie recipes actually belong to her grandmother!

Grandma Eadie. My Grandma Eadie is truly an inspiration. I won't reveal her age, but let's just say she's well past the age of making a graceful retirement. She's never let her age hold her back: today, she works five days a week as a hostess at a restaurant (a two-level restaurant, to boot), and she stops in at our shop every day for her coffee. She watches everything and keeps us in check, and customers and coworkers alike call her "Grandma Eadie." I think I got my cooking gene from her! She's graciously allowed me to share her wonderful recipe for Double Chocolate Chip Cake (page 44) with you.

Alexa & Craig Sindelar, and Alexa's mom, Amy Grescowle. Alexa, Craig, and I met back in early 2004 at a now-defunct restaurant called Pluton. Craig was the sommelier, and I worked in the pastry department. Alexa started working in pastry at Pluton just a week before I left the restaurant to pursue my dream of opening my own shop. I'll never forget Alexa's first day—she told me, "That Craig is really cute. Does he have a girlfriend?" Flash forward a few months: Alexa left Pluton to work full time for Sarah's Pastries & Candies, and she and Craig went on their first date the night before she started working with me. They've been together ever since (and now their family has grown, with the arrival of baby Kennedy), and so have Alexa and I. (Thank God for Pluton!) Alexa has been my head chocolatier and store manager from the very beginning, and today Craig is the head sommelier at Chef Grant Achatz's world-famous Alinea restaurant in Chicago. Alexa's mom, Amy Grescowle, contributed her recipes for carrot cupcakes and a fantastic cream-cheese frosting (Amy's Amazing Carrot Cupcakes and Amy's Awesome Cream Cheese Frosting, pages 55–58), and Craig created a delightful cocktail recipe for me called the Green Goddess (page 66).

The team at the French Pastry School. The French Pastry School gave me the skills, knowledge, techniques, and, most importantly, the support I needed to start my own business. I attended the school in 2003 and had the pleasure of being taught by some of the world's greatest chefs, including Jacquy Pfeiffer, Sebastien Canonne MOF, John Kraus, and Laura Ragano. The French Pastry School—and Chef Jacquy in particular—continue to support me and my business in ways I never could have imagined and for which I will always be grateful. I've based my recipes for Naked Cupcakes (page 79), Sinful Chocolate Soufflés (page 81), French Pistachio Macarons (page 94), and Vanilla Bean Chocolate Truffles (page 111) on their recipes.

PART ONE

What It Takes to Make Delicious and Beautiful Treats

My Story

Many of my favorite memories involve food. My dad was in the restaurant business in Chicago, so we were lucky enough to always be surrounded by good food. I was the middle child in my family, and food was always a central part of everyday life for my brothers and sisters and me. Even though I am notorious for having a terrible memory (I can't remember most of the things I probably should), I vividly remember the first times I laid eyes on my favorite desserts:

- I'll never forget the first time I ate a chocolate bar. It was a giant chocolate–coconut bar, actually, that friends of my parents used to send us every year during the holidays.

- My dad always kept chocolate-covered almonds stashed in the freezer, and every time he'd visit St. Louis on business, he'd bring home the most amazing molasses caramel lollipops and deep gooey butter cakes.

- On a visit to Delicias, a great restaurant in Rancho Santa Fe, California, I tried a chocolate cake that was so good, it inspired me to take my first job in a professional kitchen—just to learn how I could make it myself. In case you're wondering, the cake in question is served warm, with a cream cheese and chocolate chip center. See what I mean? It could make a pastry chef out of pretty much anybody—it's heaven on a plate.

So as I grew up, I always had an extreme love of food. Like many people who enjoy cooking, my love affair started with a love of *eating*. Food truly has the ability to make people happy, and that is why I love food. In my senior yearbook, I wrote down a couple of quotes that have pretty much defined the person I grew up to be:

> "There is no love sincerer than the love of food."
> —George Bernard Shaw

> *"Yo como, por eso soy."* ("I eat, therefore I am.")
> —Ms. Rodriguez, my somewhat less famous high school Spanish teacher, who was wise nonetheless.

Toward the end of my senior year in high school, I began to think a lot about what I wanted to do for a living. I knew that work takes up more time than any other single activity, so I wanted to do something that I would enjoy doing so work wouldn't feel like "work."

My love for eating evolved into a love of cooking when I was about nine. I was always hanging out in the kitchen. I remember a babysitter of mine, Ramon, once taught me how to make amazing nachos with refried beans. My Uncle Page taught me how to make popovers. According to my parents, aunt, uncles, and babysitters, I was always in the kitchen, making a mess.

I love the idea that something that you make with your bare hands can bring happiness and joy to you and others. In a world when nearly everything is mechanized or computerized, I think it's refreshing to make something from start to finish, to transform simple raw ingredients like flour, sugar, cocoa powder, and butter into a mouthwatering, smile-forming chocolate soufflé, and to know that you did it all by yourself—well, maybe with a little help from an electric mixer …

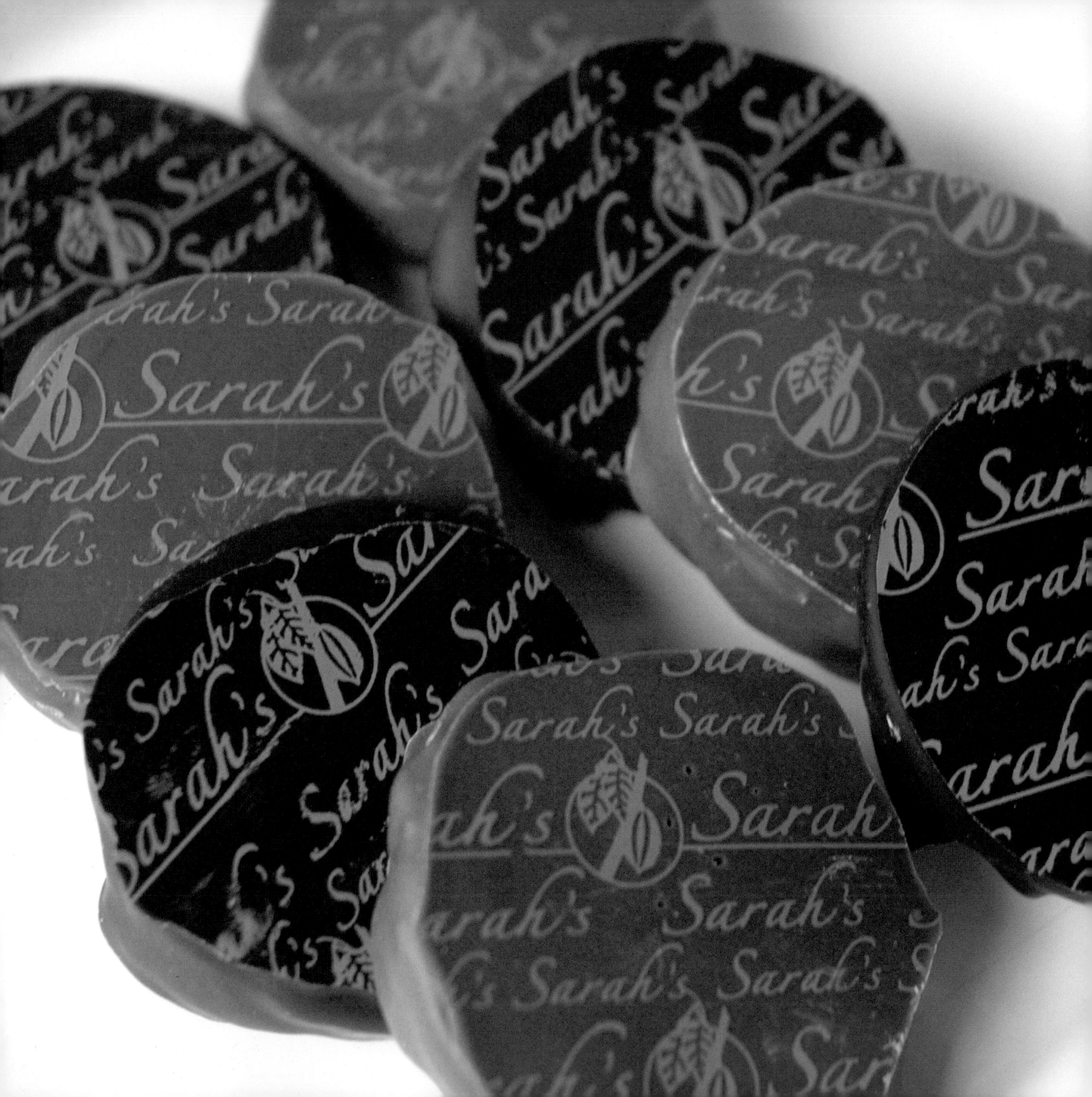
Sarah's

My Secrets

First of all, don't be intimidated by pastry. You're making this at home, so even if it doesn't look exactly like you want it to, it probably still tastes great. And remember, even if it doesn't turn out as you wanted in the taste department, you can always stop by the bakery.

If you spend a little time reading over this first section, you'll feel a lot more relaxed about making your own beautiful, delicious treats. In the pages that follow, I demystify a lot of the techniques that make sweet things taste and look really good, and I provide some useful tips to help you save time, effort, and money.

I've also included two handy charts that list major ingredients and tools used in the recipes in this book (see pages 30–33). If you see an "R" in the box, it's a required tool or ingredient; an "O" means it's optional. You can use it as a quick reference to find another use for those leftover ingredients you've got in the refrigerator or pantry.

METHODS AND TECHNIQUES

Melting chocolate in a double boiler. A double boiler is a specialized piece of kitchen equipment consisting of two fitted saucepans. The larger saucepan is partially filled with water brought to a simmer or boil (very important—the water should not touch the inner pan). The inner saucepan uses this indirect heat to melt the chocolate. This is a wise method to use for any recipe that requires extremely low heat, because it cooks items slowly and evenly. A double boiler can also be used to cook a custard, such as a lemon curd or crème

brûlée. If you don't have a true double boiler, you can use a large saucepan filled with water with a metal bowl placed on top.

Melting chocolate in a microwave. Believe it or not, the French Pastry School of Chicago advocates this method for melting chocolate. Water and chocolate are mortal enemies, so the microwave is ideal—it eliminates the possibility of water or other forms of moisture getting into the chocolate. Remember to always set your microwave at 50% power, or you may burn the chocolate. (If your microwave only works at 100% power, use the double-boiler method.) Microwaves vary greatly in strength, so make sure to start by setting your timer to only 1 minute in order to test its strength. For complete directions on melting chocolate in a microwave, see page 54.

Sifting. Flour and confectioners' sugar should always be sifted before being added to a recipe. Sifting removes impurities, breaks up clumps, and adds air to the flour, which helps produce lighter pastries.

Creaming. This is the critical process of mixing fats and sugars together until the mixture is light, fluffy, and pale in color and no grains of sugar remain. The creaming process incorporates necessary air into the mixture, which will help leaven the finished product. It is also easier to blend other ingredients into creamed butter. It is best to use an electric stand mixer fitted with the paddle attachment for creaming, but you can also use a hand mixer. Mix for about 5 to 6 minutes, scraping the sides occasionally, until the mixture is just right.

And here's some comforting news—it's pretty much impossible to overmix a creamed mixture.

Active time. In my recipes, "active time" refers to the actual active time required to prepare a recipe. Active time does not include baking or refrigeration times, as you can be doing other things while your treats are in the oven or chilling in the fridge.

Weighing ingredients. Like most pastry chefs, I always weigh my ingredients when baking because it produces a more consistent finished product. For example, a cup of freshly sifted flour can weigh as much as 25% less than a cup of flour that has sat for a while. Using weight as your guideline also protects you from worries about whether or not your ingredients were loosely spooned into a measuring cup (as they should be for flour), or densely packed into the cup (as they should be for brown sugar). I have converted all of my recipes to non-weight measurements, but you will probably find that an inexpensive kitchen scale can be a real lifesaver.

Tempering. Tempering is the process of heating or cooling chocolate in order to coat or dip an item, such as a cookie or a candy. If properly tempered, the chocolate's cocoa butter molecules are stabilized, creating a shiny, smooth chocolate with a nice "snap." At the bakery, I like to practice the traditional French table method of tempering, whereby you heat all the chocolate to 115 degrees (whether in a double boiler or a microwave) and then pour ¾ of the chocolate onto a cold slab. Granite or marble works well, but you can always use your countertop, too—just clean it beforehand with a bowl of water with a few drops of bleach in it. Work the chocolate around with a bench scraper and a large offset spatula, spreading it out in a circular motion. Repeat the steps twice in order to make sure that all the chocolate cools evenly. You will know that the molecules have crystallized when the chocolate has thickened and is cold to the touch (try dab-

bing a small amount of chocolate on the back of your wrist). Once the chocolate has cooled, scrape it back into the bowl, and the hotter chocolate will increase the temperature of the cooler chocolate. It is critical to stir it very well. To test the temper, dip a small piece of parchment paper in the tempered chocolate and set the paper down on a hard, cool surface—preferably granite or marble. Properly tempered chocolate will set up and harden within 2 to 3 minutes. If you break the piece of chocolate-dipped paper in half, it should making a snapping sound. See page 54 to explore the seeding method of tempering chocolate, which is easier to follow at home. Chocolate tempering is not to be confused with the process of tempering eggs or milk. That type of tempering involves slowly increasing the egg or milk's temperature, so it does not instantly scramble or curdle when added to a hot mixture. Eggs or milk are tempered by adding in the hot mixture to the egg/milk a spoonful at a time until the mixture is thoroughly blended.

TOOLS OF THE TRADE

Ramekins. These attractive, small, glazed ceramic serving bowls, which are usually circular with a fluted exterior, are designed to withstand the intense heat of the oven, as well as the frigid recesses of the freezer. They are frequently used to make individual-serving items like crèmes brûlées, soufflés (see page 81), and chocolate molten cakes (see page 122).

Loaf pan. For most of my recipes, I like to use a 9 × 5 inch loaf pan. Either glass or metal will do.

Silpat sheets. These nonstick pastry sheets, which were invented by baker M. Guy Demarle, ensure that baked goods come off easily after baking. See buying information on pages 27–28. They are also used for rolling out gum paste and fondant (see under Ingredients, p. 24) to make sugar decorations.

Wire rack. This is the best tool to use for cooling baked goods, because its elevated nature allows the air to circulate so that you don't end up with a soggy-bottomed treat.

Chinois. A chinois is a conical sieve with an extremely fine mesh that's often used to strain custards and sauces, such as a raspberry coulis.

Microplane hand grater. Microplane manufactures a variety of affordable handheld graters that are razor-sharp and great for finely grating citrus zest or spices.

Baking sheet. Throughout this book, you'll often see me refer to these as "sheet trays." Buy baking sheets that are heavy duty, with a 1-inch rim on all four sides. They are great for baking cookies, but you'll also find them handy for making a variety of other recipes.

Thermometer. Thermometers are a kitchen essential for countless reasons, but they are downright mandatory for any candy recipe or recipes that involve frying. I love the Pyrex Professional Digital Thermometer, which is available at Bed, Bath and Beyond and other retailers. It has a wire-attached metal probe, so it can be inserted into caramel, sugar syrup, cakes, and any other kind of food, and it displays the temperature digitally, so it's easy to read. Another plus for the Pyrex model is that it can be used as a timer, too!

Kitchen scale. I recommend picking up a digital kitchen scale, because then you'll always be confident that you have the right amount of a particular dry ingredient, or that your large eggs really are large eggs. Don't be frightened: a digital kitchen scale can be quite inexpensive (as little as $25 at Target and other retailers). My absolute favorite kitchen scale, which is made by Salter, can be found at Bed, Bath and Beyond—it can weigh items up to 11 pounds in increments as small as ⅛ ounce or 1 gram. Just in case you don't have one,

I've included a handy chart of standard weights for ingredients on pages 30–33.

Timer. Your oven has one, and your microwave just might, too. If you have the Pyrex kitchen thermometer, it includes a handy timer as well.

Mixing bowls. It's always a good idea to have a variety of different-sized mixing bowls—particularly since just one recipe could require several of them! Stainless-steel mixing bowls are perfect for slowly melting chocolate over a pot of boiling water, which is the double-boiler method. You can also choose plastic or Pyrex bowls, if that's what you prefer.

Bench scraper. This handy tool goes by many different names—pastry scraper, dough scraper, and bench knife, to name a few alternatives. It's a simple tool, usually 6 inches in length, with a straight, dull metal blade and a metal or plastic handle. Bench scrapers should be used when working with dough, and they are also my secret weapon for creating cakes with a smooth, polished look. It's also very handy for transferring finely chopped ingredients from the cutting board to their final destination.

Measuring cups. For dry ingredients, use metal or plastic "graduated" measuring cups (meaning they come as a set, in an assortment of sizes). Most dry ingredients should be spooned into graduated measuring cups and then leveled out with the handle of your spoon or a knife (the exception is brown sugar, which should always be packed into the measuring cup—but that's not really a dry ingredient anyway, is it?). For liquid ingredients, use a clear glass measuring cup, and don't forget to check the measurement at eye level for optimal accuracy.

Rubber spatula. These are great for transferring ingredients and "folding" ingredients into each other (you'll read more about that later). Ideally, you should have a large and a small spatula, so you're not stuck trying to use a large spatula to empty out a tiny peanut butter jar.

Metal offset spatula. The offset spatula, with an angled blade for accuracy, is my favorite kitchen tool because it's so versatile—great for frosting cupcakes, transferring cookies from sheet trays, and fixing "mistakes" when decorating cakes (I'll own up to using it once or twice to scrape off a misspelled name on a birthday cake). Large offset spatulas are also great for tempering chocolate (see page 18).

Pastry brush. It's pretty much what it sounds like—a food-safe version of a paint brush. Pastry brushes are used to apply simple syrup (a mixture of equal parts sugar and water that's boiled and then cooled) to cakes to help keep them moist, to coat cake pans with softened butter, to apply an egg wash (see page 131) to dough, and many other uses.

Rolling pins. These wooden pins are used to roll dough. The American version (with handles) is called a baker's pin, and the French version (smooth, without handles) is called a French pin. Baker's pins are generally used for stiffer doughs because they provide more leverage, and French pins are used with lighter doughs. Either type of pin works fine for the recipes in this book. Always be sure to put lots of flour on your rolling pin before using it on dough—otherwise, the dough will stick.

Pastry bags (aka piping bags). I love inexpensive, disposable plastic pastry bags, and here's a cost-saving tip: you can use them several times before throwing them away. Piping bags are crucial for frosting cupcakes, decorating cakes, and piping French Pistachio Macarons (see page 94). Always use a tip when using a pastry bag, and using different shaped tips can give your baking goods a more professional appearance. When using a pastry bag for detail work, like decorations on

cakes, it's wise to use both a coupler and a tip, so you can quickly slip off one tip and use a different one. A coupler is a piece of plastic that can be used to slip tips off and on without emptying the contents of the piping bag. When decorating cakes, I like to cut off about a quarter of the bag (so it doesn't get in the way when piping) and then use a white plastic coupler with two pieces (one placed inside the bag, and one that screws onto the outer part of the bag after the tip is on to keep the tip in place). With the coupler in place, you don't have to empty out the whole bag in order to switch tips. A small, round tip is great to use for writing on cookies or cakes. Another note about tips: You'll notice when you start shopping (and reading the recipes in this book) that each tip has a product number that refers to the standard size and style of the tip. For example, the ½-inch round cake decorating tip used for Rafael's Righteous Cream-Cheese Brownies (see page 41) is style #804. All tip manufacturers use the same numbers, so no matter which company's tips you choose, you'll be fine as long as you look for that style number.

Whisks. Whisks are used to blend ingredients. Nowadays, stand mixers fitted with a whisk attachment are frequently used in place of hand whisks—thus giving our poor arms a break—but back in the day, egg whites were beaten by hand for a loooong time with a balloon whisk (which is considerably wider than a standard whisk) to make meringue. It's best to use stainless steel whisks, and you'll often find them useful for blending ingredients together.

Ice cream/cookie scoop. As its name suggests, this tool has traditionally been used to remove ice cream from a carton and form it into a ball. I find it to be a useful tool for scooping cookies, and in fact some scoops are sold as cookie scoops. I like a metal 2-inch diameter scoop with a spring-action lever in the handle. When pressure is applied to the lever, it moves an arc-shaped blade across the scoop's interior and ejects the content.

*You'll need a piping bag to get an effect like the beading on this cake,
and you can achieve the smoothness of the frosting with a bench scraper.*

Food processor. This wonderful machine is similar to a blender, but it does much more. It is particularly good for grinding and chopping solids (chocolate, etc.) and cutting fats (such as butter) into dough to make pie crusts. I love the brand Robot Coupe. The company invented the food processor, and its machines are extremely well built and durable. At the pastry shop, we use our Robot Coupe to grind up the crumble topping for our Sour Cherry Pie (see page 126).

Stand mixer/hand mixer. Stand mixers make our lives easier by holding the mixing bowl steady and doing all the hard work of mixing. For almost every recipe in this book (the exception is the Chocolate–Raspberry Brioche recipe on page 130), you can substitute a hand mixer for the stand mixer. I think you'll find the stand mixer to be necessary for the brioche recipe because the mixer must knead the brioche dough for 10 to 15 minutes at high speed, and that's a long, long time to hold on to a hand mixer. Most hand mixers come with beater, whisk, and dough hook attachments. Where you are directed to use a stand mixer with a paddle attachment, use the hand mixer's beaters. When you are directed to use a stand mixer with a whisk attachment or a dough hook attachment, use the appropriate hand mixer attachment if you have it.

Knives. I recommend having at least three styles of quality knives—a chef's knife, a paring knife, and a long, serrated knife. A chef's knife is a long, broad, and heavy knife that is great for chopping and slicing. A paring knife is a small knife with a short blade and is good for tasks that require precision, such as splitting a vanilla bean in half. A serrated knife has a "teeth" on the blade and is ideal for cutting cake layers, bread, or chocolate.

Sifter or sieve. Sifters are designed to screen out any lumps or impurities in a dry ingredient. Sifters are usually metal, with a bottom made of fine mesh and a beater that moves back and forth across the mesh. You put in a dry ingredient and move the beater back and forth to push the dry ingredient out into your mixture. A sieve has a round center made of fine mesh surrounded by a wood, plastic, or metal ring. Sieves are primarily used to separate unwanted elements from dry ingredients and break up clumps. When I use a sieve instead of a sifter, I generally push the dry ingredients through the mesh material with a rubber or plastic dough scraper. You can use either tool to sift dry ingredients that require sifting.

Strainer. A specific type of sieve used to separate liquids from solids. You probably use one all the time to drain pasta.

INGREDIENTS

Dry Ingredients

All-purpose (AP), bread, pastry, and cake flour. AP flour is milled from a combination of hard and soft wheat; hard wheat is the primary component of bread flour, and soft wheat is the primary component of cake flour. The "hardness" of the wheat is directly proportional to the wheat's protein and gluten content, which means that a bread baked with bread flour is going to be tougher and higher in protein than one made with AP flour. Bread flour, which also contains a small amount of malted barley flour, tops the charts with 14% protein content. Its high gluten content makes breads especially crusty. AP flour's protein content ranges from 10 to 11%; pastry flour, which is high in starch and low in protein (thus creating a very tender product), has a 9% protein content; and cake flour, which makes the most delicate baked goods, contains only 7 to 8% protein. As for substitutions, you can use AP flour in place of bread flour, but never use bread flour in place of AP flour. If a recipe calls for pastry flour and you don't have it on hand, you can use equal parts AP and cake flour instead. By the way, a flour is called "bleached" if it is treated with bleaching chemicals to make it whiter.

Almond flour. Almond flour is just blanched whole almonds that have been ground into a fine powder. I use it in my recipes for French Pistachio Macarons (see page 94) and Naked Cupcakes (see page 79).

Baking soda. Baking soda is a dry leavening agent, which means it makes baked goods rise. It contains nothing but pure bicarbonate of soda.

Baking powder. Don't mix this one up with plain baking soda. Like baking soda, baking powder is a dry leavening agent. The difference between baking powder and baking soda is that baking powder also contains starch and cream of tartar (see below). It is used in quick breads (breads that do not require a time set aside to rise, such as muffins and waffles) instead of yeast because it instantly creates a rise action.

Table, sea, and kosher salts. The main difference among these varieties of salt is that sea and kosher salt have larger grains than table salt. Table salt's very fine granules dissolve quickly, and it also contains a small amount of calcium silicate to prevent clumping. Because of table salt's fine grains, however, 1 teaspoon of table salt is the equivalent of 1 *tablespoon* of sea or kosher salt. Ironically enough, I prefer to use sea salt for seasoning at the table because it's not processed (it's simply evaporated sea water) and has a slightly different flavor. Because it's expensive, it's important to remember that it loses that unique flavor when cooked or dissolved, so I normally reserve it for seasoning. Kosher salt does not have any preservatives and comes from either sea water or underground sources. It's frequently used when preserving foods or preseasoning before cooking because its large crystals draw moisture out of meats and other foods more effectively than other salts.

Cream of tartar. Interestingly enough, this important stabilizing agent (added to egg whites, it provides volume) is a by-product of the production of wine; it is tartaric acid that forms naturally on the tops of wine casks blended with potassium hydroxide. In sweet desserts, it adds a delicious creaminess because it inhibits the formation of crystals.

Wheat germ. Wheat germ is a concentrated source of several nutrients, including vitamin E, folic acid, phosphorous, and zinc. It contains fiber, complex carbohydrates, and protein. My Mom's Granola recipe (see page 90) calls for wheat germ. Store it in the refrigerator or freezer, and always keep it away from sunlight.

Chocolate and Chocolate Ingredients

Cocoa butter. This yellow fat extracted from the *cacao* bean (which is also the source of cocoa paste) is also called theo broma oil or theobroma cacao. It's a principal ingredient in chocolate.

Cocoa powder and cocoa liquor. Cocoa powder comes from the cocoa beans that grow in pods on the tropical theobroma cacao tree. Once the beans are fermented, dry roasted, and cracked, the nibs are ground down to extract 75% of their cocoa butter. What's left is a dark brown paste called cocoa liquor. The liquor is left to dry out again, and then the resulting hardened mass is ground into unsweetened cocoa powder. Dutch cocoa is rich and dark; the term "Dutch process" means the powder has been treated with alkali to neutralize the cocoa's natural acidity. It's best to store cocoa powder in a cool, dark place, and it will remain usable for up to 2 years.

Cocoa paste and cocoa mass. Both of these terms are used interchangeably; they refer to the pure, ground-up *cacao* (also known as cocoa) beans that turn into a paste-like substance and are used to make chocolate.

Unsweetened chocolate. Unsweetened baking chocolate is available at any supermarket—usually the Baker's brand. It's nothing but cocoa paste, pure and simple. I love to use Valrhona or Callebaut unsweetened chocolate, but those brands can be hard to find, and quite expensive. Be sure that you don't confuse unsweetened with bittersweet—they are very different types of chocolate.

Bittersweet, semisweet, dark, and milk chocolate. Dark chocolate gets its distinctive flavor from its higher concentrations of cocoa paste and cocoa butter. It consists of cocoa paste, sugar, cocoa butter, sugar, lecithin (an emulsifier), and vanilla. Dark chocolate is a generic term used to describe both semisweet and bittersweet chocolates; it's a catchall name that includes basically all chocolate except milk and white chocolate. Bittersweet chocolate must contain at least 35% cocoa paste, whereas semisweet chocolate can have between 15 and 35% cocoa paste. Often, the terms "semisweet" and "bittersweet" chocolate are used interchangeably, but semisweet chocolate usually has a higher sugar content, and thus it is usually sweeter. Milk chocolate, which has a considerably softer flavor, consists of sugar, milk powder, cocoa butter, cocoa paste, vanilla, and, sometimes, lecithin.

Couverture chocolate. Couverture is a high-quality type of chocolate with a cocoa butter content that is higher than other chocolate, with a minimum of 32% cocoa paste content. Also, to be considered couverture, the combined cocoa butter and cocoa paste content must be greater than 54%. The remaining percentage is sugar. Therefore, a 64% chocolate has a combined cocoa butter and cocoa paste content of 64%, and the remaining 36% of the mixture is sugar—so the higher the percentage of cocoa, the more bitter the chocolate. Couverture chocolate is shinier, creamier, and crisper, which means that if it is tempered correctly and placed on a piece of parchment paper to set up, you will hear a snap when you break it in half.

White chocolate. This one is the subject of considerable debate; because it contains no cocoa paste, many don't consider it to be chocolate at all. It contains sugar, cocoa butter, milk powder, lecithin, and vanilla.

Chocolate pistoles. Pistoles are coin-shaped pieces of chocolate commonly used in cooking and baking.

Lecithin. Lecithin, an ingredient in many types of chocolate, is an all-natural emulsifier, or a substance that helps ingredients that don't naturally want to mix (like oil and water).

Decorating Materials

Gum paste. This dough, which is made with glucose syrup (see page 26), confectioners' sugar, and gums, is extremely pliable—it is as malleable as the Play-Doh of your youth, in fact. Because of its sugar content, gum paste dries hard and crispy, and it can be very brittle. It is used to make beautiful pastry decorations, especially flowers. It is edible, but it is quite bland.

Fondant. Fondant is a white sugar-based mixture that has myriad uses in baking and candy making; it is used for purposes as diverse as the cream filling in a chocolate-covered cherry and the smooth, perfect, and tint-ready surface of a wedding cake. It can be rolled, poured, or sculpted.

Marzipan. Made from ground almonds and sugar, this modeling paste is used to make edible decorations.

Other Must-Have Ingredients

Granulated, confectioners', light brown, and dark brown sugar and glucose syrup. Granulated sugar, of course, is the stuff

ANNA BLESSING

With chocolate, quality is very important—
cheap chocolate just doesn't taste as good.

you put in your coffee (or at least some people do). Confectioners' sugar (also known as powdered sugar) is the tasty stuff that looks like snow that you see dusted over goodies. The difference between light and dark brown sugar is that dark brown sugar contains more molasses, a by-product of the processing of sugar beets or cane sugar, and thus the flavor is more intense. As I mentioned earlier, white sugars should be loosely spooned into measuring cups, and brown sugars should always be densely packed. Glucose syrup, a sweetener usually processed from wheat, corn, grapes, or honey, which has a similar consistency to corn syrup, has 50% of the sweetening power of granulated sugar. It's great to use when making caramel to help prevent the sugar from crystallizing. Because it is very hard to find for home cooks, I recommend substituting light (but not lite, which is low calorie) corn syrup for the recipes here in *Sweetness*. Glucose syrup is extremely sticky and can be hard to work with, so it helps to heat the measured glucose for around 10 seconds in the microwave before pouring it into your mixture; you'll be glad you did. You can buy Wilton's brand, which is made with corn, quite inexpensively online at the Wilton website or at Amazon.com. A wheat-based alternative is available at Pastry Chef Central (www.pastrychef.com).

Large eggs. I always recommend using large eggs in recipes because it's the standard size of a chicken egg in the United States. On average, a whole large egg weighs 50 grams (the yolk weighs 20 grams and the white weighs 30 grams)—and it's not a bad idea to test the weight of your large eggs on your kitchen scale before dumping them into a recipe. An oversized egg or two can make a difference in your recipe. All baking recipes require warming eggs to room temperature.

Unsalted butter. Always use unsalted butter when making the recipes in this book, because you can always add salt to taste on your own. My favorite brand of butter is Plugra, because of its high fat content. You can find Plugra in the dairy case at many grocery and specialty stores (including Whole Foods and Super Target stores). All baking recipes require warming butter to room temperature except those that specifically require cold (pie crust leaps to mind) or melted butter. For the majority of my recipes, I've indicated in the Prep section of each of my recipes that you should set out your butter (and your eggs, if applicable) a couple of hours before making your recipes, but if you forget, you can place the butter in your microwave at 50% power for three separate 20-second increments to achieve the same result.

Yeast. This amazing one-celled fungus converts sugar and starch into carbon dioxide bubbles and alcohol—and that chemical miracle makes baked goods rise. Without yeast, there would be no crusty breads, beer, or wine. There are many varieties of yeast used in baking, but the most common are compressed bakers' yeast and active dry yeast. Most commercial bread is made with compressed bakers' yeast, which creates lots of bubbles that become trapped in the dough. Those bubbles make the bread rise, so it's light and airy when baked. A small amount of alcohol is also produced, but it burns off as the bread bakes. Compressed bakers' yeast works faster and longer than active dry yeast, but it's very perishable and loses potency a few weeks after it's packed. It's popular among commercial bakers, but home bakers usually prefer dry yeast. To use compressed bakers' yeast, dissolve a cake of the yeast in a liquid that's warmed to 70° to 80°F. You can store it in the refrigerator, well wrapped, for 3 weeks, or in the freezer for up to four months. If you freeze it, defrost it for a day in the refrigerator before using it. Substitutions: 1 package or 2¼ teaspoons of active dry or compressed baker's yeast for each 0.6-ounce cake of compressed bakers' yeast; or 2¼ teaspoons of bread machine yeast for each 0.6-ounce cake of compressed bakers' yeast. You should be able to find compressed bakers' yeast, which is sold in soft taupe-colored blocks, in the dairy cooler at your supermarket.

Flavorants

Vanilla extract. Simply indispensable. I just love the Nielsen-Massey brand.

Vanilla paste. This is a sweet, concentrated vanilla extract that has vanilla bean seeds included in the mix. It is very useful in recipes where you don't want to add much additional liquid. Again, Nielsen-Massey makes the best.

Nut butters. Nope, there's no butter in them at all. Nut butters are easy to make yourself—they're just roasted nuts, vegetable oil, salt, and a little sugar mixed in a blender or food processor until smooth.

Praline paste. This delicious concoction is a mixture of almond or hazelnut butter and sugar. It can be hard to find, but it is available at King Arthur Flour's website (see next section).

Feuilletine. These crispy crushed wafer pieces add a delicious crunch to ganache (see page 111), candies, cakes, and pastries. In a pinch, you can substitute crushed corn flakes or crispy rice cereal in many recipes, if crispness is what you're going for, but it won't taste the same.

SHOPPING

In order for your recipes to turn out perfectly, it's important to take the time to find the correct ingredients and tools. Trust me: your efforts will be worth it!

Ingredients

Pastry Chef Central (www.pastrychef.com): The same company listed previously for baking tools is also a great resource for tough-to-find ingredients, such as cocoa butter, couverture chocolate, glucose syrup, cocoa powder, edible gold leaves, hazelnut praline paste, almond flour, vanilla bean paste, feuilletine, and fondant.

King Arthur Flour (www.kingarthurflour.com): This company carries a wide variety of flours, naturally, and other hard-to-find fine ingredients, such as chocolate (truly wonderful brands, such as Barry Callebaut, Belcolade, and Guittard), and the wonderful Nielsen-Massey line of vanilla, chocolate, orange, lemon, and almond extracts. You can also purchase Nielsen-Massey's vanilla bean paste and whole vanilla beans.

Nielsen-Massey Vanilla (www.nielsenmassey.com) and Callebaut Chocolate (www.callebaut.com): You can't buy Nielsen-Massey vanilla products or Callebaut chocolate on the companies' sites, but you can learn about their entire line of products, find great recipes, and get fantastic tips on techniques like tempering, decorating, and more. Purchase Nielsen-Massey vanilla products and Callebaut chocolate at sites like Amazon, King Arthur Flour, and other retailers.

Baking Tools

Kerekeds (www.bakedeco.com): This company's great website features bakeware, cookware, pans, mixers, knives, and more.

JB Prince (www.jbprince.com): This company is dedicated to serving most pastry needs and has items like sheet trays, scales, spatulas, cutters, Silpat mats, and anything else you might imagine.

Wilton (www.wilton.com): Wilton has long been a leader in cake decorating, and their site is a one-stop shop for all of your baking needs. Among its myriad items are every kind of pastry-bag tip imaginable. Wilton's site is also a reliable place to find glucose syrup.

Demarle (www.demarleusa.com): Demarle was the inventor of the Silpat mat, and the company also makes wonderful Flexipan molds (rubber molds used to make petit fours and other pastries) that will release your treats with ease.

Pastry Chef Central (www.pastrychef.com): This is a one-stop source for gold cake boards, blow torches (for finishing off crèmes brûlées), chocolate dipping forks, cake pans, kitchen scales, flour sifters, offset spatulas, pastry bags, pastry tips, cake stands (for frosting cakes), acetate ribbons, and acetate sheets, among other useful items.

Amazon (www.amazon.com): After you do your research at these and other sites, you might find that Amazon is a fan-tastic resource for many tools (and many of the ingredients, too, for that matter). Its prices are often tough to beat, and its policy of offering free shipping on purchases over $25 might save you even more in the long run.

WHAT YOU'LL NEED

Refer to the charts of ingredients and tools provided on pages 30–33 to quickly determine whether or not you have on hand the items you'll need for a recipe you're planning to make. If you see an "R" in the box, it's a required tool or ingredient; an "O" means it's optional. If more than one of the items is required for a recipe, you'll see a number next to the "R."

STANDARD WEIGHT CHART

Don't worry—*you're* not going to have to get on a scale after eating any of these treats. This is a great reference chart so you can make sure you're accurately measuring your ingredients. One of the best tricks for making recipes turn out flawlessly is using a kitchen scale. In particular, I like to weigh my dry ingredients instead of measuring them in cups, tablespoons, and teaspoons, because it is much more accurate and consistent.

First, a note about grams, ounces, and pounds: There are 28.35 grams in an ounce, 16 ounces in a pound, and 454 grams in a pound.

ITEM	VOLUME	OUNCES	GRAMS
Almond flour	1 cup	3.35	95
Almonds, slivered	1 cup	3.81	108
Baking powder	1 tablespoon	0.49	13.8
Baking soda	1 tablespoon	0.49	13.8
Blueberries, fresh	1 cup	5.11	145
Butter (1 stick)	8 tablespoons	3.92	111
Carrots, grated	1 cup	3.88	110
Cream cheese, roughly 1 package	1 cup	8	227
Chocolate, unsweetened, grated	1 cup	4.66	132
Chocolate, unsweetened, melted	1 cup	6	170
Cinnamon, ground	1 tablespoon	0.25	7

ITEM	VOLUME	OUNCES	GRAMS
Cocoa powder, unsweetened	1 cup	3.03	86
Coconut, sweetened, shredded	1 cup	3.28	93
Corn starch	1 tablespoon	0.28	8
Corn syrup, light	½ cup	11.57	328
Cream, heavy whipping (fluid)	1 cup (yields 2 cups whipped cream)	8.1	238
Cream, light whipping (fluid)	1 cup (yields 2 cups whipped cream)	8.1	238
Cream of tartar	1 teaspoon	0.11	3
Egg white, large	1 egg white	1	30
Egg, whole, large	1 whole egg	1.75	50
Egg yolk, large	1 egg yolk	0.75	20
Flour, all-purpose, unsifted	1 cup	4.5	127
Flour, bread, unsifted	1 cup	4.83	137
Flour, cake, unsifted	1 cup	3.75	106
Ginger, ground	1 tablespoon	0.19	5.4
Glucose syrup	1 cup	—	—
Jam	1 tablespoon	0.71	20
Milk, skim	1 cup	8	227
Milk, whole	1 cup	8.5	244
Molasses	1 cup	12	337
Oil, vegetable	1 cup	7.69	218
Peanut butter, chunky, with salt	1 cup	9.1	258
Peanut butter, smooth, with salt	1 cup	9.1	258
Pecans, chopped	1 cup	3.84	109
Raisins, packed	1 cup	5.82	165
Raspberries, fresh	1 cup	4.34	123
Rice, puffed	1 cup	0.49	14
Salt	1 tablespoon	0.66	19
Strawberries, fresh, sliced	1 cup	5.86	166
Sugar, brown, densely packed	1 cup	7.76	225
Sugar, granulated	1 cup	7.05	200
Sugar, confectioners', sifted	1 cup	3.53	100
Vanilla extract	1 tablespoon	0.5	14
Water	1 cup	8	227

"R" = a required tool or ingredient. If more than one of the items is required for a recipe, you'll see a number next to the "R."

"O" = an optional tool or ingredient.

Recipe	All-Purpose Flour	Vegetable Oil	Corn Starch	Cream	Unsalted Butter	Eggs	Chocolate	Granulated Sugar	Vanilla Extract	Salt	Vanilla Beans	Confectioners' Sugar	Brown Sugar
Mom's Almond Moon Cookies	R				R							R	
Rafael's Righteous Cream Cheese Brownies	R				R	R		R	R	R			
Grandma Eadie's Double Chocolate Chip Cake			R		R	R		R					
Holiday Vanilla Bean Sugar Cookies	R				R	R			R		R		R
Royal Icing						R						R	
Decadent Chocolate-Covered Strawberries							R						
Amy's Amazing Carrot Cupcakes	R	R			R	R		R	R	R			
Amy's Awesome Cream Cheese Frosting								R	R			R	
Supreme Chocolate Cupcakes					R	R			R	R			
Chocolate Buttercream Frosting					R	R	R	R	R				
Green Goddess									R				
Mom's Fudge Brownie Sundae	R				R	R	R	R	R	R			
Black-and-White Cupcake Batter					R	R			R	R			
Fantastically Fudgy Vanilla and Cocoa Icing				R			R		R	R	R	R	
Naked Cupcakes					R	R			R			R	
Sinful Chocolate Soufflés			R		R	R			R	R		R	
Banana–Chocolate Chip Pound Cake	R				R	R	R	R	R				
Mom's Granola													
French Pistachio Macarons		R						R					
Rafael's Pistachio Buttercream Filling					R	R			R				
Bittersweet Chocolate Chip Cookies	R				R	R	R	R	R	R			R
Decadent Chocolate–Almond Toffee					R		R	R	R		R		
Raspberry Pepin Jam									R	R			
Rafael's Toffee Sugar Cookies	R				R	R			R	R			R
Vanilla Bean Chocolate Truffles				R			R	R			R		
Lemon Baby Rattle Cookies	R				R	R			R	R	R	R	
Rafael's Coconut–Apricot Macaroons						R			R		R		
Chocolate Molten Cakes					R			R				R	
Sour Cherry Pie	R		R		R	R		R	R				R
Chocolate–Raspberry Brioche	R				R	R	R	R	R				
Uncle Page's Popovers	R				R	R			R				

Recipe	Glucose Syrup	Corn Syrup	Milk	Honey	Baking Powder	Baking Soda	Raisins	Cocoa Powder	Food Processor	Blender	Piping Bags and Tips	Paring Knife	Pyrex Bowl
Mom's Almond Moon Cookies													
Rafael's Righteous Cream Cheese Brownies											R	R	R
Grandma Eadie's Double Chocolate Chip Cake													
Holiday Vanilla Bean Sugar Cookies												R	
Royal Icing											R	R	
Decadent Chocolate-Covered Strawberries													R
Amy's Amazing Carrot Cupcakes					R	R							
Amy's Awesome Cream Cheese Frosting													
Supreme Chocolate Cupcakes					R	R		R					
Chocolate Buttercream Frosting											R		
Green Goddess										R		R	
Mom's Fudge Brownie Sundae												R	
Black-and-White Cupcake Batter			R		R						R (2)		
Fantastically Fudgy Vanilla and Cocoa Icing	O	R											
Naked Cupcakes						R							
Sinful Chocolate Soufflés			R					R					
Banana–Chocolate Chip Pound Cake					R	R							
Mom's Granola													
French Pistachio Macarons	O	R		R					R		R (2)		
Rafael's Pistachio Buttercream Filling													
Bittersweet Chocolate Chip Cookies						R							
Decadent Chocolate Almond Toffee	O	R							O				R
Raspberry Pepin Jam													
Rafael's Toffee Sugar Cookies					R				O				
Vanilla Bean Chocolate Truffles	O	R						R					
Lemon Baby Rattle Cookies									R			R	
Rafael's Coconut–Apricot Macaroons		R											
Chocolate Molten Cakes													R
Sour Cherry Pie													
Chocolate–Raspberry Brioche													
Uncle Page's Popovers			R										R

"R" = a required tool or ingredient. If more than one of the items is required for a recipe, you'll see a number next to the "R."

"O" = an optional tool or ingredient.

	GRATER	PEELER	SPATULA	OFFSET SPATULA	WHISK	SIFTER	WIRE RACK	MELON BALLER	FINE STRAINER	PASTRY BRUSH	COOKIE SCOOP	COOKIE CUTTERS
Mom's Almond Moon Cookies			R			R	R				R	
Rafael's Righteous Cream Cheese Brownies						R	R					
Grandma Eadie's Double Chocolate Chip Cake			R			R	R					
Holiday Vanilla Bean Sugar Cookies						R	R					R
Royal Icing					R	R	R					
Decadent Chocolate-Covered Strawberries												
Amy's Amazing Carrot Cupcakes	R		R		R	R	R					
Amy's Awesome Cream Cheese Frosting						R						
Supreme Chocolate Cupcakes						R						
Chocolate Buttercream Frosting					R	R						
Green Goddess		O										
Mom's Fudge Brownie Sundae						R	R					
Black-and-White Cupcake Batter						R		R				
Fantastically Fudgy Vanilla and Cocoa Icing				R (2)		R						
Naked Cupcakes						R	R	R		R		
Sinful Chocolate Soufflés						R	R			R		
Banana–Chocolate Chip Pound Cake						R						
Mom's Granola												
French Pistachio Macarons					R	R	R					
Rafael's Pistachio Buttercream Filling			R									
Bittersweet Chocolate Chip Cookies						R	R				R	
Decadent Chocolate–Almond Toffee					R	R						
Raspberry Pepin Jam												
Rafael's Toffee Sugar Cookies												R
Vanilla Bean Chocolate Truffles					R				R			
Lemon Baby Rattle Cookies							R					R
Rafael's Coconut–Apricot Macaroons											R	
Chocolate Molten Cakes						R	R					
Sour Cherry Pie						R		R				
Chocolate–Raspberry Brioche					R			R		R		
Uncle Page's Popovers						R	R					

	Parchment Paper	Baking Sheet	Bundt Pan	Thermometer	Ramekins	Cupcake Pan	Cupcake Liners	Pie Pan	Gloves	Rolling Pin	Hand Mixer	Stand Mixer
Mom's Almond Moon Cookies		R (2)										
Rafael's Righteous Cream Cheese Brownies		R (2)									R	O
Grandma Eadie's Double Chocolate Chip Cake			R								R	O
Holiday Vanilla Bean Sugar Cookies	R	R (2)								R	R	O
Royal Icing											R	O
Decadent Chocolate-Covered Strawberries	R	R (2)		R								
Amy's Amazing Carrot Cupcakes						R (2)	R					
Amy's Awesome Cream Cheese Frosting											R	O
Supreme Chocolate Cupcakes						R (2)	R					
Chocolate Buttercream Frosting				R							R	O
Green Goddess												
Mom's Fudge Brownie Sundae		R									R	O
Black-and-White Cupcake Batter						R (2)	R				R	O
Fantastically Fudgy Vanilla and Cocoa Icing				R							R	O
Naked Cupcakes						R						
Sinful Chocolate Soufflés					R						R	O
Banana–Chocolate Chip Pound Cake											R	O
Mom's Granola		R (2)										
French Pistachio Macarons	R	R (2)		R							R	O
Rafael's Pistachio Buttercream Filling				R							R	O
Bittersweet Chocolate Chip Cookies	R	R (2)									R	O
Decadent Chocolate–Almond Toffee	R	R (2)		R					R			
Raspberry Pepin Jam				R								
Rafael's Toffee Sugar Cookies		R (2)								R	R	O
Vanilla Bean Chocolate Truffles	R	R (2)		R					R			
Lemon Baby Rattle Cookies	R	R (2)								R	R	
Rafael's Coconut–Apricot Macaroons	R	R (2)		R								
Chocolate Molten Cakes					R	R (2)	R				R	O
Sour Cherry Pie								R		R	R	O
Chocolate–Raspberry Brioche				R	R (2)	R (2)					R	R
Uncle Page's Popovers						R						

PART TWO The Recipes

Work

Most people spend more of their waking hours at work than in any other single place, so why not make it as enjoyable as possible? In this section, you will find solutions for many of the unique social dilemmas of the workplace—from the perfect birthday present for your boss to an afternoon snack that could save your sanity.

- **Mom's Almond Moon Cookies**
- **Rafael's Righteous Cream Cheese Brownies**
- **Grandma Eadie's Double Chocolate Chip Cake**
- **Holiday Vanilla Bean Sugar Cookies**
- **Royal Icing**

Whip up that absolutely necessary afternoon snack

ACTIVE TIME 30 minutes

YIELD About 28 cookies

PREP

Take your butter out of the refrigerator a couple of hours before you make the dish.

Preheat the oven to 325°F.

Grease 2 baking sheets.

Clean out some space in your fridge so you can place the dough balls on the baking sheets in it before baking.

Sift the confectioners' sugar and the flour.

Toast and chop the almonds.

INGREDIENT FINDER

Slivered almonds are the best kind to use for this recipe. You can find packages of them in the produce section of most supermarkets, and you can buy them in bulk at Whole Foods stores.

You can find Nielsen-Massey vanilla extract at Williams-Sonoma stores.

GRAB THESE

Sifter

Stand mixer fitted with the paddle attachment or a hand mixer

2 greased baking sheets

Cookie scoop (1½-inch diameter)

Spatula

Knife or food processor

Wire rack

SHELF LIFE AND STORAGE INSTRUCTIONS

10 days at room temperature in a sealed airtight container; dough can be stored for as long as 2 months in the freezer (see page 45 for instructions)

Do you feel sluggish in the late afternoon? These **almond moon cookies** will give you just the jolt you need. You can even make a batch and leave them in your desk (they have a 10-day shelf life).

My mom has been making these melt-in-your-mouth cookies for my siblings and me since I can remember. I am the middle child in a family of five children, which often meant fending for myself. I'd do just that—starting with hiding handfuls of these cookies in my dresser drawer.

BREAKING IT DOWN

Originally, my mom made these as crescent moon–shaped cookies, but by the time she'd had her fourth child, there never seemed to be enough hours in the day. Spending time with a cookie cutter just didn't seem prudent, so my mom went for full moon–shaped cookies instead, by shaping them into balls.

You can use a small (1½-inch) diameter cookie or ice cream scoop (see page 20) to help speed along the shaping process.

This cookie dough can be kept for 2 months in the freezer. Follow the cookie dough freezing instructions on page 45.

You can vary how finely you chop the almonds, depending on your preference for a smoother, more finely ground cookie, or one with chunks of almonds (that's how I like them).

 # Mom's Almond Moon Cookies

INGREDIENTS	QUANTITY
Unsalted butter, warmed to room temperature	2 sticks (16 tablespoons)
Confectioners' sugar, sifted	¼ cup, plus roughly 1 cup for coating the cookies after they're baked
All-purpose flour, sifted	2 cups
Vanilla extract (I recommend Nielsen-Massey brand)	1 teaspoon
Almonds, slivered, finely chopped	1 cup

Preheat the oven to 325°F.

1. In the bowl of a stand mixer fitted with the paddle attachment, or in a mixing bowl (if using a hand mixer), cream the butter until it is light and fluffy.

2. With the mixer still running, slowly add in the ¼ cup confectioners' sugar and the flour, mixing until well combined.

3. With the mixer still running, add in the vanilla extract. Turn off the mixer, and slowly add the chopped almonds. Mix until the almonds are just combined, about 1 minute.

4. Use the cookie scoop to scoop out balls of dough, and place the balls 2 inches apart on the prepared baking sheets. Try not to touch the dough balls, as doing so will warm the dough.

5. Bake at 325°F for about 30 minutes, or until the bottoms are lightly brown.

6. Cool the cookies completely on a wire rack. Pour the remaining 1 cup confectioners' sugar into a low bowl and roll the cooled cookies around in it until covered.

Just the right thing for your boss's birthday

ACTIVE TIME 30 minutes

YIELD About 36 brownies

PREP
Take your eggs, butter, and cream cheese out of the refrigerator a couple of hours before you make the dish.

Preheat the oven to 300°F.

Grease two 9 × 5-inch baking pans.

Assemble the piping bag, coupler, and tip (see page 20).

INGREDIENT FINDER
You can find Baker's brand unsweetened chocolate at most supermarkets.

GRAB THESE
Sifter

Double boiler (see page 17) or microwave

Whisk

Stand mixer fitted with the paddle attachment or a hand mixer

Two 9 × 5-inch greased pans

Piping bag fitted with ½-inch round tip (#804)

Paring knife

SHELF LIFE AND STORAGE INSTRUCTIONS
4–5 days refrigerated in a sealed airtight container

How do you properly thank the person responsible for putting food on your table? With the gift of brownies, of course. A batch of luscious **Rafael's Righteous Cream Cheese Brownies** will put even the grumpiest of bosses in a good mood with its creamy, slightly tangy cream-cheese center and perfectly rich dark-chocolate swirl. They will stay fresh for several days if properly refrigerated and kept in a sealed container or bag, so it's also a gift that keeps on giving. Make sure you allow plenty of time for these brownies, as you'll need to allow them to cool completely at room temperature and then refrigerate them for 4 to 5 hours before slicing the brownies.

BREAKING IT DOWN

My family has been friends with the Schulmans, owners of the famous Chicago institution Eli's Cheesecake, since—*forever*. When I first opened my pastry shop, Maureen Schulman made me look her straight in the eye and promise I would *never make cheesecake*.

Well, I never break a promise. Our genius head pastry chef, Rafael Ornelas, created this delicious cream cheese brownie recipe, and it's the closest we will *ever* come to making cheesecake.

Rafael's Righteous Cream Cheese Brownies

INGREDIENTS	QUANTITY
Unsalted butter, warmed to room temperature	2 sticks (8 tablespoons)
Unsweetened chocolate (I recommend Valrhona or Callebaut, but Baker's brand is much easier to find)	¾ cup (3⅓ ounces)
Granulated sugar	3 cups, divided
All-purpose flour, sifted	½ cup
Whole eggs, warmed to room temperature	6 large, divided
Salt	¼ teaspoon
Vanilla extract	2 teaspoons
Cream cheese, warmed to room temperature	2½ packages

Preheat the oven to 300°F.

1. Melt together the butter and chocolate in a double boiler (see page 17) or microwave (see page 54). Transfer to a large mixing bowl.

2. Using a whisk, blend 2 cups of the sugar and the salt into the chocolate–butter mixture.

3. Slowly add 4 of the eggs to the mixture, 1 at a time.

4. In 3 separate batches, add in the flour.

5. Add the vanilla.

6. In the bowl of a stand mixer fitted with the paddle attachment, or in a mixing bowl (if using a hand mixer), beat together the cream cheese and remaining 1 cup sugar until smooth (about 2 minutes), and then add the remaining 2 eggs, 1 at a time. (For this step, it is best to use a stand mixer fitted with the paddle attachment, but you can use a regular mixing bowl and a hand mixer if necessary.)

7. Measure out 1½ cups of the chocolate mixture and set aside to use as a topping.

8. Pour the remaining chocolate mixture into the greased 9 × 5-inch pans.

9. Spread the cream cheese mixture on top of the chocolate mixture.

10. Fill the piping bag fitted with the #804 tip with the reserved chocolate mixture. Pipe lines along the width of the brownies, about 1 inch apart.

11. Run the paring knife through the length of the brownies (in the opposite direction of the piped lines you created), creating a pretty streaking effect. You can also use the knife to make "swirls" of whatever design you would like.

12. Bake at 300°F for 50 to 60 minutes. Cool completely in the pans. After they cool completely at room temperature, refrigerate them in the pans for at least 4 to 5 hours before slicing.

Send your coworker off right with chocolate cake

ACTIVE TIME 20 minutes

YIELD 1 Bundt cake

PREP

Take your eggs out of the refrigerator a couple of hours before you make the dish.

Preheat the oven to 350°F.

Prepare a Bundt pan using a pastry brush to coat it with butter, or spray it with butter-flavored Pam, just like my grandma does.

INGREDIENT FINDER

The cake and chocolate pudding mixes are easy to find at your local supermarket—no fancy food store needed!

GRAB THESE

Bundt pan

Stand mixer fitted with the whisk attachment or a hand mixer

Spatula

Wire rack

SHELF LIFE AND STORAGE INSTRUCTIONS

2 days at room temperature in a sealed airtight container.

It would be rude to ignore the fact that someone you have worked alongside for the past year is moving on to bigger and better things. My **Grandma Eadie's double chocolate chip cake** is so delicious, your coworkers will think it took you hours to make! It's our little secret that this is one of the easiest recipes out there, and you can even "cheat" a little bit by purchasing some ready-made ingredients.

BREAKING IT DOWN

This old-fashioned recipe can be jazzed up by using the highest-quality chocolate chips you can find. Because I love dark chocolate, I recommend using bittersweet chocolate chips, but you can also use milk chocolate. You could also get *really* crazy and throw in some butterscotch chips.

 # Grandma Eadie's Double Chocolate Chip Cake

INGREDIENTS	QUANTITY
Pillsbury Moist Supreme Devil's Food Cake mix	1 (18.25-ounce) package
Royal Instant Pudding & Pie Filling mix, chocolate	1 (5.5-ounce) package
Water	¾ cup
Vegetable oil	¾ cup
Sour cream	¾ cup
Whole eggs, warmed to room temperature	4 large
Miniature chocolate chips	12 ounces

Preheat the oven to 350°F.

1. In the bowl of a stand mixer fitted with the whisk attachment, or in a mixing bowl (if using a hand mixer), combine all the ingredients, except the chocolate chips.

2. Mix on medium speed for 8 minutes.

3. Using a spatula, fold in the chocolate chips.

4. Pour the batter into the greased Bundt pan.

5. Bake at 350°F for 50 minutes.

6. Let cool in the pan for 5 minutes, and then invert onto a wire rack to cool completely.

Make the season bright at the office with cookies

ACTIVE TIME 1½ hours

YIELD About 24 cookies

PREP

Take your eggs and butter out of the refrigerator a couple of hours before you make the dough.

Sift the confectioners' sugar and the flour.

Preheat the oven to 350°F.

Line 2 baking sheets with parchment paper.

INGREDIENT FINDER

The website Copper Gifts (www.coppergifts.com) offers a wide variety of cookie cutters. The truly adventurous might want to consider a custom cookie cutter, which is a particularly nice option for gift-giving. The company Kitchen Collectibles can make custom-made cookie cutters with nothing more than a simple hand drawing that you supply. Visit the company's site at http://kitchengifts.com/custom.html to learn more.

Some places to find whole vanilla beans include Trader Joe's, World Market, Whole Foods, and Costco. You can also cheat and use vanilla bean paste (see page 27); 1 tablespoon of paste is the equivalent one of 1 whole vanilla bean.

GRAB THESE

Sifter

Holiday cookie cutters (Christmas trees, snowmen, dreidels, etc.)

Paring knife

Parchment paper

2 baking sheets lined with parchment paper

Rolling pin

Marble slab (or just clean off the kitchen counter with water mixed with a few drops of bleach), for rolling out dough

Stand mixer fitted with the paddle attachment or a hand mixer

Wire rack

SHELF LIFE AND STORAGE INSTRUCTIONS

7 days at room temperature in a sealed airtight container; dough can be stored for as long as 3 months in the freezer (see Breaking It Down at right for instructions) or 3 to 4 days in the refrigerator.

Instead of ordering overpriced and underloved cookies from a supermarket, excite the office bunch by making them yourself! These **holiday vanilla bean sugar cookies** not only look beautiful—they taste delicious too! Pick up a box of cute holiday cookie cutters and get rolling—the dough, that is!

BREAKING IT DOWN

Chef Rafael Ornelas figured out that when making the Royal Icing (see page 48) that coats these cookies, using a stand mixer's paddle attachment works much better than the whisk attachment because it incorporates less air, thus creating fewer air bubbles. Fewer air bubbles means dipping the sugar cookies will be much easier, and the cookies will be prettier. But don't worry: if you don't happen to have a stand mixer, a hand mixer works just fine.

This cookie dough can be stored in the freezer for as long as 3 months—and believe me, it will come in handy when you have a last-minute cookie emergency or a simple sweet-tooth craving in the wee hours of the night. To freeze the dough, roll it into a log, wrap it in plastic wrap, and place it in a ziplock bag or another airtight container.

Holiday Vanilla Bean Sugar Cookies

INGREDIENTS	QUANTITY
Vanilla bean	1
Unsalted butter, warmed to room temperature	3 sticks plus 5 tablespoons (29 tablespoons)
Salt	¼ teaspoon
Confectioners' sugar, sifted	1¾ cups
Egg yolks, warmed to room temperature (save the whites for the Royal Icing!)	2 large
All-purpose flour, sifted	3¾ cups
Royal Icing (see recipe on page 48)	1 recipe

Preheat the oven to 350°F.

1. Extract the vanilla bean seeds from each bean pod: Using a paring knife, split the bean in half, and use the blunt side of the knife to scrape out the seeds. Set the seeds aside and discard the pods, or stick them in a jar of sugar to make vanilla sugar.

2. In the bowl of a stand mixer fitted with the paddle attachment, or in a mixing bowl (if using a hand mixer), cream together the butter, salt, and vanilla bean seeds.

3. As the mixer continues to run, add in the confectioners' sugar, mixing thoroughly. Then, slowly add in the egg yolks, 1 at a time.

4. Stop the mixer, scrape the bowl, and turn the mixer back on. Then, slowly add in the sifted flour, ½ to ¼ cup at a time, until just combined (and you can't see any traces of the flour).

5. Cover the dough and refrigerate for at least 1 hour.

6. Remove the dough from the bowl. Lightly flour your work surface, and using a rolling pin, roll the dough into a disk about ½-inch thick. With your cookie cutters, cut out the cookies and place them 2 inches apart on the prepared baking sheets. Continue until you have used all the dough. If the dough becomes too soft, you may need to refrigerate it again for a bit. You want the dough to be quite firm while you work with it.

7. Bake at 350°F for 12 minutes, or until the bottoms are golden brown.

8. Let the cookies cool on a wire rack for 20 minutes (if you are in a rush, you can pop them in the refrigerator for about 10 minutes).

9. Decorate the cookies with Royal Icing (see recipe and instructions on page 48).

You've made the cookies—now, make 'em beautiful!

ACTIVE TIME 15 minutes

YIELD 3 cups

PREP

Take your eggs out of the refrigerator a couple of hours before you make the icing. If you've made the icing for the vanilla bean sugar cookies, use the two leftover egg whites!

Sift the confectioners' sugar.

Juice the lemon.

Assemble the piping bag, coupler, and tip (see page 20).

INGREDIENT FINDER

You can find food coloring at the supermarket or at fine food stores; I prefer gel food color, and Americolor and Chefmaster are my favorite brands.

You can find the decorative sprinkles, sanding sugar, and dragees shown in the photograph on page 46 at Sur La Table.

GRAB THESE

Sifter

Stand mixer fitted with the paddle attachment or a hand mixer

Offset spatula

Paring knife

6-quart mixing bowl

Food coloring, if desired

Baking sheet

Piping bag fitted with #3 round tip

Wire rack

SHELF LIFE AND STORAGE INSTRUCTIONS

5 days refrigerated in a sealed airtight container

Decorating sugar cookies with my delicious **Royal Icing** is one of my favorite things to do. I find the "dipping" part to be very relaxing, and the more detailed decorating part allows my creativity to flow. Of course, it's also fun to see—and eat—the finished product.

BREAKING IT DOWN

The consistency of the Royal Icing on these delicious cookies can be easily altered by adding sifted confectioners' sugar, to make it thicker, or room-temperature water, to make it thinner. If you plan to dip your cookies, the icing should be slightly thinner, and if you are decorating the cookies with a piping bag (see opposite page for decorating with a piping bag, including writing on the cookies), it is better to make the mixture thicker. Also, be sure you strain the lemon juice before adding it to the mixture, so none of the seeds gets into the icing.

 # Royal Icing

INGREDIENTS	QUANTITY
Egg whites, warmed to room temperature	4 large
Confectioners' sugar, sifted	4 cups
Lemon juice	2 teaspoons

1. In the bowl of a stand mixer fitted with the paddle attachment, or in a mixing bowl (if using a hand mixer), combine all ingredients and mix on medium speed until glossy, about 5 minutes.

TO ADD COLOR TO THE ICING:

1. Separate the icing into two batches—¾ of the mixture in one bowl to use as the dipping icing, and ¼ of the mixture in another bowl to use as the piped icing. If you want the cookies to be dipped in different colors of icing, separate your dipping icing again into enough bowls that you have one for each color you desire. Squirt 1 to 2 drops of food coloring into each bowl as desired. Use a rubber spatula to thoroughly blend each drop of color into the frosting before adding more. Add the color to your personal preference, and remember, it's always a good idea to have white food coloring on hand in case you add too much of one of the colors. If you don't have white food coloring, you could also reserve some pure white icing before you begin adding colors so you can add it if needed. Here's a tip: Always keep a cup of clean water while you work with the different colors of frosting so you can wash your spatulas before moving among the colors.

2. Add the water to the dipping mixture until it reaches the desired thickness. You can test the consistency by dipping a cookie in it and placing it on a baking sheet. The icing should be thin enough to ensure that you can see a trace of icing on the cookie, but not so thin that it runs off the sides of the cookie. If you have added too much water, you can thicken it with more sifted powered sugar.

3. Mix food coloring, 1 drop at a time, into the reserved ¼ mixture of the icing until the desired color is reached. After testing to make sure it is of the desired consistency, transfer this icing for writing on or decorating your cookies into the piping bag (see Step 3 below).

TO DECORATE COOKIES:

1. Pick up a cookie and dust off any crumbs, so they won't "dirty" the icing.

2. Holding the cookie in one hand by all 5 fingertips, dip 1 side of the face-down cookie into the icing. Spin the cookie around on the tips of your fingers to ensure that the frosting covers the entire surface area. Pull the cookie up and out of the icing, and jiggle your wrist to shake off excess icing. Wipe off any excess icing against the side of the bowl. Using an offset spatula or small paring knife, pop any air bubbles that remain and eliminate any imperfections.

3. Place the dipped cookies on a sheet tray. Let the icing dry. Fit a disposable piping bag with a coupler and a #3 round tip, and fill it halfway with the icing. If you are right-handed, place the bag with the icing in your right hand and use your left index finger to guide your right hand as you draw. Practice on a piece of parchment paper to make sure that the icing is stiff enough to keep the lines intact. Holding the bag at a 90-degree angle, apply gentle pressure to the piping bag with your right hand, allowing the icing to fall out of the bag and onto the cookies. Try writing names or placing polka dots or flowers on the cookies. To achieve the look shown in the photograph on page 46, use a pastry bag to pipe the Royal Icing onto the cookie, and while the icing is still wet, dip the cookie into a plate containing sanding sugar or sprinkles. The wet icing will make them stick to the cookie.

Social Gatherings

The right baked good can turn any social gathering into a real treat (no pun intended). Ease the anxiety of meeting his parents with chocolate-covered strawberries; they'll know that you'll treat their son with as much care and attention to detail as you have the strawberries. Or spice up a low-key night at home with freshly baked cupcakes. Pretty soon, you won't be able to show up anywhere without baked goods in tow!

- **Decadent Chocolate-Covered Strawberries**
- **Amy's Amazing Carrot Cupcakes**
- **Amy's Awesome Cream Cheese Frosting**
- **Supreme Chocolate Cupcakes**
- **Chocolate Buttercream Frosting**
- **Green Goddess**

ANNA BLESSING

Showing his parents a very berry good time

ACTIVE TIME 45 minutes

YIELD
24 chocolate-covered strawberries

PREP
Let the strawberries warm to room temperature by removing them from the fridge about 2 hours before you prepare them. If you're in a pinch, you can use a blow dryer (preferably one that has not touched your hair) to warm up the strawberries.

Line 2 baking sheets with parchment paper.

Wash and dry the strawberries.

INGREDIENT FINDER
Believe it or not, it can be challenging to find an old-school heating pad without a cloth cover—but you'll be glad you did. The plastic cover makes it much easier to clean. Try Target or Walgreens.

Candy thermometers are surprisingly inexpensive (as low as $10) and can be found at Target and similar stores.

GRAB THESE
Pyrex bowl (for melting chocolate)

Candy thermometer

Cutting board and chef's knife

2 baking sheets

Parchment paper

Marble slab (or just clean off the kitchen counter with water mixed with a few drops of bleach)

Heating pad

SHELF LIFE AND STORAGE INSTRUCTIONS
2 days in a refrigerator.

Meeting the parents for the first time? Show off your attention to detail by blowing them away with these **decadent chocolate-covered strawberries**. They'll know that the concentration and hard work you've expended on this fantastic treat will transfer to other areas of your life. This recipe is ideal to prepare in the spring, when fresh strawberries are in their prime.

For an even more elegant look, use a piping bag to drizzle white choolate over the strawberries, as shown in the photograph on page 51.

BREAKING IT DOWN

I prefer heating chocolate in the microwave, since water and chocolate are enemies and the double-boiler method (see page 17) brings with it a greater chance that the water and chocolate will come in contact with each other. Also, the microwave method is faster and dirties fewer dishes.

If you are dipping more than a few dozen strawberries (or if you get carried away and begin dipping everything you can find in your pantry in chocolate—believe me, stranger things have happened), place the bowl of chocolate on a heating pad, set to medium, and stir occasionally to evenly distribute the heat. This will ensure that the chocolate will stay warm and won't harden.

You should never use frozen strawberries in this recipe (they are too soggy), but you can use any kind of chocolate you like, from milk chocolate to my favorite, dark chocolate.

The key to producing shiny and decadent-looking chocolate-covered strawberries is making sure that you temper your chocolate before dipping. Tempering creates a smooth, lustrous, and shiny chocolate with a nice, crispy "snap." Tempering is the process of stabilizing the cocoa butter molecules in the chocolate. There are several methods to tempering chocolate, including the traditional French table tempering method we use at our shop (see page 18), but I recommend the seeding method (see page 54) when tempering at home, as it requires fewer tools and less time. Also, keep in mind that if you don't temper the chocolate, it will still taste delicious; it just won't look as pretty. So if you are ever having a chocolate-covered strawberry craving of your own, there's no need to temper!

The ultimate test of a good temper is to dip a small piece of parchment paper in your tempered chocolate. It should harden within 3 minutes. When you break it in half, you should hear a loud snap, indicating that the chocolate has been properly tempered. The chocolate should appear shiny and smooth.

Decadent Chocolate-Covered Strawberries

INGREDIENTS	QUANTITY
Dark chocolate (64%) pistoles or bar, divided	2 pounds
Fresh strawberries, warmed to room temperature	24
White chocolate	3 ounces (about 6 pieces of a bar)

1. Temper the chocolate using the seeding method, as follows. Either use chocolate pistoles (see page 24) or finely chop the chocolate.

2. Heat 1½ pounds of the chocolate either in the microwave at 50% power for about 3 minutes (in 1 minute increments) or in a double-boiler. After each minute in the microwave, stir the chocolate thoroughly; you will probably find that this hastens the melting process and minimizes the amount of the time it needs to spend in the microwave. Bring the temperature of the melted chocolate to 113 to 122°F. Set about a third of the melted chocolate aside and slowly add the remaining half pound of solid chocolate to the larger portion of the melted chocolate, thereby reducing the temperature of the hot chocolate, and stir with a spatula for a few minutes. Then, add the remaining third of melted chocolate until it is all melted, uniform in texture, and has reached 90°F. Keep the melted chocolate warm by setting it on a heating pad (see page 53 for details).

3. Test your tempering skills by dipping a small piece of parchment paper into the chocolate. Place the paper on a cold, hard surface (like a granite or marble countertop or slab). The chocolate should completely "set up" and harden within 3 minutes, and it should appear shiny and smooth. Break it in half to make sure it's properly tempered; you should hear a loud "snap" when it breaks.

4. Now, the fun part. Keep your chocolate in a bowl and hold each strawberry by its stem. Dip each strawberry into the chocolate, about ¾ of the way. Shake off any excess (is that really possible?) chocolate by flicking your wrist back and forth. Place each chocolate-covered strawberry on the parchment-lined baking sheet when finished.

5. Place the strawberries into the refrigerator for about 30 minutes. (Ideally, chocolate should be placed in a room with the temperature set at 60°F, but if you don't happen to have a chocolate room on hand, the refrigerator will do.)

6. If you're like me and don't think there's such a thing as having too much chocolate on your chocolate-covered strawberries, you can dip the chocolate covered strawberries again and again, until the chocolate is all used up (we find that two dips per strawberry is just right). If you don't use it all, remember to save any excess chocolate—you can pour it out onto a parchment-lined baking sheet, wait for it to set up, and then chop it into small pieces and place in an airtight container for later reuse.

7. Once the chocolate has set up, melt the white chocolate for about 45 seconds in a microwave at 50% power. Using a spoon held about 1 foot above the strawberries, drizzle the white chocolate up and down on the strawberries, making white stripes. Remember, it's all in the wrist, so try to move your hand back and forth rapidly to keep the lines looking fragile. Another way to keep the lines delicate is to raise the bag at least 4 inches above the strawberry.

8. Store the strawberries in the refrigerator.

The appropriate reward for your favorite team!

ACTIVE TIME 30 minutes

YIELD 12 cupcakes

PREP

Take your eggs out of the refrigerator a couple of hours before you make the dish.

Sift the flour.

Fill the cupcake trays with paper cupcake liners.

Preheat the oven to 350°F.

INGREDIENT FINDER

All of the ingredients are commonly available at any supermarket—no trip to a specialty food store needed!

GRAB THESE

Sifter

2 cupcake pans

Paper cupcake liners

Box grater

Rubber spatula

Stand mixer fitted with the whisk attachment or a hand mixer

Offset spatula

SHELF LIFE AND STORAGE INSTRUCTIONS

2 days refrigerated in a sealed airtight container

You're never too old to play for a mediocre sports team—it keeps the child inside you alive (my personal favorite is kickball). One particular day, my team was feeling pretty low, so I tried to energize them with **Amy's Amazing Carrot Cupcakes**. Unfortunately, they were beyond help. When that failed, I decided to give the cupcakes to the referee instead—much to my teammates' relief.

This recipe is a family recipe, but it's not from my family. Alexa Sindelar is the head chocolate maker and store manager at Sarah's Pastries & Candies, and this recipe is from her mom, Amy Grescowle.

BREAKING IT DOWN

There is always much debate as to whether this should be called a carrot *muffin* or carrot *cupcake*. I guess we call it a cupcake because it's frosted, but if the "C word" makes you feel guilty, just call it a muffin (and just think, after eating one of these, you've probably fulfilled your vegetable quota for the day).

These lovelies rise high in the oven, so fill each baking cup only halfway.

If you want a little more pep in your step, increase the amount of spices, but just remember, a little goes a long way.

A friend of my mine tested this recipe using preshredded carrots, and it just didn't turn out the same way. I recommend that you freshly grate your own carrots. If you have a food processor at home, you can cut the carrots into large "chunks" (about 3 × 2 inches) and let the food processor do the dirty work!

Amy's Amazing Carrot Cupcakes

INGREDIENTS	QUANTITY
Carrots, peeled and grated	1½ cups, tightly packed (5¼ ounces; about 1½ medium carrots)
All-purpose flour, sifted	1¼ cups
Granulated sugar	1 cup
Baking powder	1 teaspoon
Baking soda	1 teaspoon
Cinnamon, ground	1 teaspoon
Nutmeg, ground	⅛ teaspoon
Salt	Pinch (1/16 teaspoon)
Vegetable oil	¾ cup
Whole eggs, warmed to room temperature	3 large
Vanilla extract	¼ teaspoon
Pecan pieces, untoasted (optional)	½ cup
Amy's Awesome Cream Cheese Frosting (see recipe on page 58)	1 recipe

Preheat the oven to 350°F.

1. Shred the carrots using a box grater. Set aside.

2. In the bowl of a stand mixer fitted with the whisk attachment, or in a mixing bowl (if using a hand mixer), combine all the dry ingredients, including the spices. Then, add the oil and eggs to the mixture. Mix well on medium speed until thoroughly combined.

3. Add the vanilla extract. Slowly add the pecans and carrots to the mixture.

4. Transfer the mixture to the lined cupcake pans, filling each liner about halfway. Bake at 350°F for about 20 minutes.

5. Let the cupcakes cool at room temperature for about 15 minutes.

6. After the cupcakes have cooled completely, using an offset spatula, frost each cupcake with Amy's Awesome Cream Cheese Frosting (see recipe on page 58).

Creamy goodness for those yummy carrot cupcakes

ACTIVE TIME

15 minutes

YIELD

Enough frosting for 12 cupcakes

PREP

Take your cream cheese and butter out of the refrigerator a couple of hours before you make the frosting, or warm them slightly in the microwave (see instructions on page 26).

Sift the confectioners' sugar.

INGREDIENT FINDER

All of the ingredients are easily found at any supermarket.

GRAB THESE

Sifter

Stand mixer fitted with the paddle attachment or a hand mixer

SHELF LIFE AND STORAGE INSTRUCTIONS

2 weeks refrigerated in a sealed airtight container

This **cream cheese frosting** is so delicious, it shouldn't just be used to top cupcakes. It also makes a great filling for cakes.

BREAKING IT DOWN

The two secrets to getting a lump-free frosting are sifting the confectioners' sugar and making sure that the cream cheese and butter warm to room temperate before mixing. If you don't have the time to allow this to happen *au naturel,* soften your cream cheese and butter by warming them in the microwave, 15 seconds at a time, at 50% power (every microwave is different, so start at 20% power just to make sure you don't end up with a pool of melted butter).

Here's another fun fact: this recipe will stay perfectly fresh stored in an airtight container in the refrigerator for as long as 2 weeks. Technically, it has the same shelf life as cream cheese (and just think how long you can leave cream cheese in the fridge!)

Chef Rafael's Tip: To make a really creamy, lump-free frosting, cream the powdered sugar with the butter for 2 minutes with 2 tablespoons of the cream cheese. Then add the rest of the cream cheese.

 # Amy's Awesome Cream Cheese Frosting

INGREDIENTS	QUANTITY
Cream cheese, warmed to room temperature	8 ounces (1 package)
Unsalted butter, warmed to room temperature	4 tablespoons (½ stick)
Vanilla extract	2 teaspoons
Confectioners' sugar, sifted	1¾ cups (½ pound)

1. In the bowl of a stand mixer fitted with the paddle attachment, or in a mixing bowl (if using a hand mixer), mix all of the ingredients together.

ANNA BLESSING

A four-bite treat that's perfect for a girls' night in ...

ACTIVE TIME

30 minutes

YIELD

12 cupcakes

PREP

Take your eggs and butter out of the refrigerator a couple of hours before you make the dish.

Sift the cake flour.

Boil the water.

Preheat the oven to 350°F.

Fill the cupcake trays with paper cupcake liners.

INGREDIENT FINDER

Cake flour is usually sold in boxes placed near the bags of all-purpose flour in the baking section of your supermarket.

GRAB THESE

Hand mixer

2 cupcake trays

Paper cupcake liners

Piping bag fitted with ½-inch star-shaped tip (#27)

SHELF LIFE AND STORAGE INSTRUCTIONS

1 day at room temperature in a sealed airtight container (they won't go bad after a day, but they won't taste as fresh and delicious as they do on that first day).

Getting together with the girls to watch your favorite guilty-pleasure TV show? Watching the latest drama unwind doesn't get any more indulgent than when it's accompanied by a fresh batch of sinfully delicious **supreme chocolate cupcakes**!

BREAKING IT DOWN

The key to a delicious cupcake is quite simple—serve it the same day it's baked! This is one item that doesn't taste as good on the second day.

Our head pastry chef, Rafael Ornelas, has finally perfected this recipe. Can you guess how he transformed this chocolate cake recipe from great to outstanding? By adding more butter, thus proving my theory that butter makes everything taste better!

 # Supreme Chocolate Cupcakes

INGREDIENTS	QUANTITY
Cocoa powder	⅔ cup
Water, boiling	⅓ cup (put a full 1 cup of water on to boil, and once it reaches the boiling point, pour ⅓ cup of the water back into a glass measuring cup and discard the remaining water)
Cake flour	1 cup, scant
Granulated sugar	1¼ cups
Baking powder	2⅛ teaspoons
Salt	¾ teaspoon
Unsalted butter, warmed to room temperature	1½ sticks (12 tablespoons)
Whole eggs, warmed to room temperature	3 large
Vanilla extract	1 tablespoon plus ½ teaspoon
Chocolate Buttercream Frosting (see page 64)	1 recipe

Preheat the oven to 350°F.

1. In a mixing bowl, combine the cocoa powder and boiling water and let cool to room temperature. Transfer to a large measuring cup.

2. In a separate mixing bowl, mix together the dry ingredients for 30 seconds. Set aside.

3. In a third mixing bowl, gently mix together the eggs and the vanilla extract. Add a third of the cocoa mixture to the egg–vanilla mixture.

4. Add the remaining cocoa mixture and the butter to the dry-ingredient mixture and mix together for 1½ minutes.

5. Add the cocoa–egg mixture to the cocoa–dry ingredient mixture in 2 separate stages, mixing for 30 seconds between each addition. Scrape the bowl to ensure that all of the cocoa–egg mixture has been added.

6. Fill each cupcake liner ¾ of the way full with batter.

7. Bake at 350°F for 20 minutes (I always recommend slightly underbaking cupcakes because it makes them even more moist).

8. Allow the cupcakes to cool completely before frosting (about 20 minutes).

9. Frost the cupcakes with Chocolate Buttercream Frosting (see recipe on page 64).

ANNA BLESSING

A luscious frosting for a luscious cupcake

ACTIVE TIME 40 minutes

YIELD Enough to frost 12 cupcakes

PREP

Take your eggs and butter out of the refrigerator a couple of hours before you make the frosting.

INGREDIENT FINDER

The best thermometer is available at Bed, Bath, and Beyond. It's called Pyrex Professional and reads the temperature in both Celsius and Fahrenheit. My favorite feature is its alarm function, which alerts you when your product has reached the desired temperature.

GRAB THESE

Candy thermometer

Stand mixer fitted with the whisk attachment or a hand mixer (it's a lot easier with the stand mixer)

Offset spatula or piping bag fitted with ½-inch star-shaped tip (#27)

SHELF LIFE AND STORAGE INSTRUCTIONS

7 days, stored in the refrigerator.

There are two types of people in the world: those who like sugary icing, and those who appreciate the lusciousness of a great Italian buttercream frosting. I fall into the latter. Sugary icing (so sugary you can feel the granules on your tongue) can be appropriate for young children (or any time your inner child comes out to play), but it's buttercream frosting, with its silky texture and rich buttery flavor, that leaves me dreaming about it hours after my last bite.

BREAKING IT DOWN

This buttercream recipe is easily adaptable to different flavors. To make a milk chocolate buttercream, substitute your favorite milk chocolate for the dark chocolate specified in this recipe (I love the Felchlin 38% brand). You can make vanilla buttercream by simply omitting the chocolate.

Make sure you keep an eye on the egg whites. Remember, once you start whipping the whites, you can't stop until you've added the butter. Otherwise, they'll deflate, and you'll have to start over.

To test that you've made a creamy and smooth buttercream, rub a small amount of it between your thumb and index finger. You shouldn't feel any graininess from the sugar.

 # Chocolate Buttercream Frosting

INGREDIENTS	QUANTITY
Granulated sugar	1⅓ cups
Water	⅓ cup
Egg whites, warmed to room temperature	4 large
Salt	Pinch (1/16 teaspoon)
Butter, warmed to room temperature	6 sticks
Dark chocolate (I prefer 64%)	¾ pound

1. In a medium saucepan over medium heat, mix together the sugar and water to 144°F to make a sugar syrup.

2. While your sugar–water mixture is heating, in the bowl of a stand mixer fitted with the whisk attachment, or in a mixing bowl (if using a hand mixer), whisk the egg whites with the salt on medium speed until they become frothy (but not yet to the point where they stiffen into peaks).

3. Turn the mixer's speed to high and slowly pour the sugar syrup over the lightly beaten whites. Turn the mixer's speed down to medium, and let the mixture cool to room temperature. The mixture should have the consistency of meringue.

4. Gradually add the room temperature butter to the mixture. This will thicken the mixture and make it appear more like the buttercream that we know and love.

5. Melt your chocolate using a double boiler, or in the microwave at 50% power (see page 17 for details).

6. Add the melted chocolate to the mixture on low speed.

HOW TO FROST THE CUPCAKES:

1. Now the fun part—frosting the cupcakes! You can use an offset spatula to spread the frosting or fill a piping bag with the frosting and fit it with a star-shaped tip (#27), to create a more elegant finish.

Note: At Sarah's Pastries & Candies, we add a little something extra by filling the center of each cupcake with frosting. To fill the center, brace the cupcake with one hand and pierce its top with the tip of the piping bag. Squeeze the piping bag to release the buttercream while simultaneously pulling the bag up and out of the cupcake. Repeat with each cupcake. After you have filled all of the centers, clean off the tip and frost the tops of each cupcake, starting at the outside of the cupcake and circling inward until finishing at the center.

Make your cocktail party a memorable occasion

ACTIVE TIME   20 minutes

YIELD   Six 8-ounce glasses

PREP

Wash the grapes and cucumbers, and peel the cucumber.

INGREDIENT FINDER

Craig recommends Collins glasses, which are 8–12 ounce narrow tumblers.

St. Germain is a French liqueur made from elderflowers. You can find it in better liquor stores.

GRAB THESE

Paring knife (for peeling and cutting cucumber)

Peeler (or you can use a paring knife)

Blender

Collins glasses

Ice

SHELF LIFE AND STORAGE INSTRUCTIONS

2 days (but it will be gone much sooner than that!)

Here's the thing about cocktail parties: They always *sound* like a good idea. But then the guests arrive. And they're thirsty. And suddenly you're stuck in the kitchen squeezing limes and scooping ice and generally ignoring the people you threw the party to hang out with in the first place.

The solution? A batch of cocktails that you can make ahead of time. That's why I asked my good friend Craig Sindelar, the head sommelier at the world-famous Alinea restaurant in Chicago, to come up with a cocktail I could make by the pitcherful! The result is the incredibly refreshing (and pretty) **Green Goddess**. The only problem? It goes down easy—very easy—so you'd better make two batches.

BREAKING IT DOWN

My favorite blanco tequila is Don Julio Blanco. My dad has been enjoying it straight up and chilled for as long I can remember. Every now and again, I can down a shot myself, but I prefer Craig's more gulpable concoction.

 # Green Goddess

INGREDIENTS	QUANTITY
Green seedless grapes	48 ounces (roughly one bunch; reserve a few grapes for garnish)
Seedless cucumber	1 medium (reserve a few slices for garnish)
Kosher salt (optional)	⅛ teaspoon
Lime juice	3 medium limes
Good-quality tequila blanco	12 ounces
St. Germain liqueur	6 ounces

1. Wash the grapes and the cucumber. Peel and slice the cucumber. Reserve a few grapes and slices of cucumber for garnish.

2. Place the grapes and cucumber into a blender and blend together until smooth. Strain the mixture.

3. Season the mixture with kosher salt (optional).

4. Add the tequila, St. Germain, and lime juice. Stir, and pour into Collins glasses filled with ice.

5. Garnish each Collins glass with a few cucumber slices and/or grapes.

Matters of Love

During my freshman year at Northwestern University, I took a
sociology class. One day, the teaching assistant asked each of us
to share our desired career path with the class. Eyes opened and
heads tilted when I spoke up and broke the trend of future doctors,
lawyers, social workers, and politicians.

"You want to own a pastry shop?" she asked, astounded.
"Well, you know what they say—the way to a man's heart is through
his belly."

It wasn't exactly the response I was looking for, but it just
might hold some truth. After all, what man has time to argue when
there's a warm chocolate soufflé sitting in front of him, screaming
to be eaten before it gets deflated and cold?

- **Mom's Fudge Brownie Sundae**
- **Black-and-White Cupcake Batter**
- **Fantastically Fudgy Vanilla and Cocoa Icing**
- **Naked Cupcakes**
- **Sinful Chocolate Soufflés**

ANNA BLESSING

Fudge brownie and ice cream—a match made in heaven

ACTIVE TIME

30 minutes

YIELD

About 18 brownies

PREP

Take your eggs out of the refrigerator a couple of hours before you make the dish.

Toast your walnuts in the oven for about 12–15 minutes.

Preheat the oven to 350°F.

Grease a 9 × 5-inch baking pan.

INGREDIENT FINDER

You can find Baker's brand unsweetened chocolate at most supermarkets. I recommend Valrhona or Callebaut chocolate.

GRAB THESE

Sifter

Double boiler (see page 17) or microwave

Whisk

Stand mixer fitted with the whisk attachment or a hand mixer

One 9 × 5-inch greased pan

Paring knife

Cutting board

Chef's knife

SHELF LIFE AND STORAGE INSTRUCTIONS

4–5 days refrigerated in a sealed airtight container.

There's nothing better than chewy and nutty **fudge brownie sundaes**, and my mom's fudge brownie recipe is particularly good. If you don't care for nuts, you can easily omit the walnuts in this recipe. We make them without nuts at the shop because we have so many other items with nuts, and my mom never fails to say, "That's not my recipe!" With or without nuts, it's a perfectly fudgy brownie—not too gooey, not too cakey.

BREAKING IT DOWN

Okay, so maybe there is one thing better than my Mom's brownies—those brownies with ice cream on top! Load up this sundae with ice cream, fudge sauce, whipped cream, nuts, sprinkles, and fresh fruit.

Don't forget to warm up the brownie before making your sundae, and I recommend using Häagen Dazs or Ben & Jerry's vanilla ice cream and the Barefoot Contessa's fudge sauce.

 # Mom's Fudge Brownie Sundae

INGREDIENTS	QUANTITY
Unsalted butter	2 sticks (16 tablespoons)
Unsweetened chocolate	4 ounces
Granulated sugar	2 cups
All-purpose flour	1½ cups
Whole eggs	4 large
Salt	¼ teaspoon
Vanilla extract	2 teaspoons
Walnuts, toasted and coarsely chopped	1½ cups

Preheat the oven to 350°F.

1. Melt the butter and chocolate together in a double boiler or microwave (see page 17). Transfer the chocolate–butter mixture to a large mixing bowl or the bowl of a stand mixer.

2. Use a cutting board and chef's knife to coarsely chop the toasted walnuts.

3. Using either the whisk attachment of a stand mixer or a hand mixer on medium speed, mix the sugar and salt into the chocolate–butter mixture while it is still hot.

4. In four alternating batches, add the flour and eggs (one at a time) into the chocolate–butter mixture with the mixer running on medium speed.

5. Add the vanilla until it is thoroughly combined.

6. Bake the brownies at 350°F for 25 to 30 minutes, or until firm throughout.

7. Let the brownies cool and then cut into 2-inch squares. Add desired toppings and serve.

A dessert you and your honey can make together

ACTIVE TIME 30 minutes

YIELD 24 cupcakes

PREP

Take your eggs and butter out of the refrigerator a couple of hours before you make the batter.

Line 2 cupcake pans with paper liners.

Preheat the oven to 350°F.

INGREDIENT FINDER

You should be able to easily find these ingredients at any supermarket.

GRAB THESE

Hand mixer

Whisk

2 cupcake pans

Paper cupcake liners

Wire rack

2 piping bags fitted with round tips (#8)

SHELF LIFE AND STORAGE INSTRUCTIONS

These are best eaten the day they're baked, but the batter will last for 2 days, so you can bake some now, and more later! The cupcakes will still taste good on the second day, but they just won't be as moist.

It's always nice to feel needed, so why not get your honey hooked on **black and white cupcakes**? These delicious treats require two people to simultaneously pour white and chocolate cake batter into the cupcake liners, so grab him and head into the kitchen. As usual, you'll be indispensable!

BREAKING IT DOWN

A friend once told me that the secret to making delicious and moist cupcakes is to slightly underbake them, so say goodbye to the toothpick test!

And don't worry—if you don't have someone to help you make these, simply fill the baking cups with one batter at a time. The cupcakes won't have clearly defined lines between the black and white parts, but they'll be delicious nonetheless.

 # Black-and-White Cupcake Batter

INGREDIENTS	QUANTITY
For the white cake batter:	
Cake flour	1½ cups plus 3 tablespoons
Baking powder	2 teaspoons
Granulated sugar	1 cup
Unsalted butter, warmed to room temperature	1 stick (8 tablespoons)
Whole milk	¾ cup
Egg whites, warmed to room temperature	3 large
Vanilla extract	1½ teaspoons
For the chocolate cake batter:	
Supreme Chocolate Cupcakes batter (see page 61)	½ recipe
For the icing:	
Fantastically Fudgy Cocoa and Vanilla Icing (see page 75)	1 recipe

Preheat the oven to 350°F.

1. Combine the flour, baking powder, and sugar in a large mixing bowl and mix briefly.

2. Add the butter and roughly 75% of the milk to the dry ingredient mixture and mix on low speed until the butter is thoroughly incorporated.

3. Increase the mixer's speed to medium and beat until well combined. Then continue to beat at medium speed for 1½ minutes longer in order to build the cake's structure.

4. In a separate bowl, lightly whisk the egg whites by hand to incorporate considerable air into the mixture. Whisk the whites until they are frothy (but not so long that soft peaks form).

5. Combine the remaining milk, the egg whites, and the vanilla into a small mixing bowl and add it in 3 separate batches to the batter, mixing well between each addition.

6. Prepare the Supreme Chocolate Cupcakes batter recipe (be sure you reduce all ingredients by half, since you only need half of the recipe to make the black and white cupcakes).

7. Once you have prepared both the white and chocolate cake batters, fill 2 piping bags fitted with round #8 tips until they are ½ full (see page 20 for further details). One bag should contain the white batter, and the other should contain the chocolate batter.

8. Prepare the cupcake pans.

9. It's important to pipe both cupcake batters simultaneously, so ask your honey to hold one of the bags. Each of you should begin to pipe the batter at the same time, filling each liner until it is ¾ full.*

10. Bake at 350°F for 25 minutes.

11. Cool on a wire rack.

12. Ice your cupcakes with Fantastically Fudgy Vanilla and Cocoa Icing.

* Tip: In order to synchronize your piping, try counting to five together as you pipe.

And now, for the icing on the (cup)cake

ACTIVE TIME

30 minutes

YIELD

Enough to coat 24 cupcakes

PREP

Take your butter out of the refrigerator a couple of hours before you plan to make the icing.

INGREDIENT FINDER

You should be able to find all the ingredients at the supermarket.

GRAB THESE

Sifter

Digital candy thermometer

Stand mixer fitted with paddle attachment or a hand mixer

2 offset spatulas

SHELF LIFE AND STORAGE INSTRUCTIONS

10 days stored in the refrigerator.

Remember my earlier point about two kinds of people in the world: those who like sugary icing and those who like buttercream? Well, this **fudgy vanilla and cocoa icing** is definitely sugary, but because we only use a thin layer on our cupcakes, it's just heavenly. The icing gets its name because its texture is so similar to that of fudge.

BREAKING IT DOWN

Maintaining the right temperature for this frosting is the key to making it easily spreadable, so make sure that the frosting always stays warm (roughly body temperature, or about 90°F). If the frosting becomes cold, you can rewarm it either in the microwave (in 20-second increments at 50% power) or over a double boiler.

If you don't have a digital candy thermometer, you can determine whether the sugar syrup is finished and at the "soft ball" stage (239°F) by dropping a spoonful of the sugar syrup into a glass of very cold water. Next, gather the syrup into a ball using your fingers. If the syrup forms into a ball while in the cold water, but flattens out when at room temperature, it's reached the "soft ball" stage.

 # Fantastically Fudgy Vanilla and Cocoa Icing

INGREDIENTS	QUANTITY
Granulated sugar	2½ cups
Corn syrup	¼ cup
Heavy whipping cream	½ cup
Salt	½ teaspoon
Unsalted butter, warmed to room temperature	1 stick plus 1 tablespoon (9 tablespoons)
Confectioners' sugar, sifted	1½ cups
Vanilla extract	1 tablespoon
Cocoa powder	½ cup

1. Combine the granulated sugar, corn syrup, whipping cream, and salt in a saucepan and cook on medium heat until the sugar syrup mixture reaches 239°F. Remove from heat.

2. In the bowl of a stand mixer fitted with the paddle attachment, or in a mixing bowl (if using a hand mixer), mix together the butter and sifted confectioners' sugar on medium speed.

3. Slow the mixer to low speed, and slowly add the sugar syrup mixture to the butter–sugar mixture.

4. Increase the mixer speed to medium-high and pour in the vanilla. Continue beating the mixture until the icing is smooth and spreadable.

5. Pour half of the mixture into a separate covered container and set aside. That's your vanilla fudge icing.

6. Add the cocoa powder to the remaining mixture still in the mixing bowl and mix thoroughly, making the cocoa fudge icing.

7. You should spread the icing on the black-and-white cupcakes while it is still warm, but the cupcakes themselves should be thoroughly cooled. Frosting the cupcakes, like piping the batter, is best done as a team effort. Using offset spatulas, one person should spread the cocoa fudge icing while the other spreads the vanilla fudge frosting. Start by making 2 separate lines of the white and black frosting down the center of each cupcake, and use the offset spatulas to spread the respective colors around each cupcake half, making sure to cover the edges.

ACTIVE TIME

30 minutes plus at least 20 minutes (preferably overnight) for the batter to chill

YIELD   6 cupcakes

PREP

Take your eggs and butter out of the refrigerator a couple of hours before you plan to prepare the batter.

Prepare the batter the night before you plan to bake the cupcakes, so it can chill overnight in the refrigerator.

Preheat the oven to 350°F.

Sift the dry ingredients together.

INGREDIENT FINDER

A chinois is a very fine strainer—nothing's getting through that thing. You can buy them at specialty stores, such as Sur La Table, but any fine mesh strainer will work.

Almond flour (see page 23) is just ground-up blanched almonds. If you can't find it in stores, just buy slivered almonds and grind them yourself in a food processor or spice grinder—or the old fashioned way, with a mortar and pestle.

GRAB THESE

Sifter

Whisk

Chinois or other fine mesh strainer

Wire rack

Cupcake pans

SHELF LIFE AND STORAGE INSTRUCTIONS

Store in an airtight container for 2 to 3 days at room temperature. The cupcakes can also be frozen for up to 6 months.

The **naked cupcake** is perfect for a girl who has just realized she is going to be keeping her clothes *on* for a while! This chocolate–almond cupcake topped with fresh raspberries is not too sweet and stays fresh for two days. The cupcakes also freeze well, in case you plan on eating dessert solo for a while.

This recipe comes from the French Pastry School, the culinary school I attended. It is actually a recipe for a traditional French petit four called a *financier* (pronounced FIN-AHN-si-ay). When I first opened my pastry shop, I couldn't understand why my cute little chocolate–raspberry *financiers* weren't selling. After I decided to make them six times larger and changed the name to *naked cupcakes* (since they don't have any frosting), they started to sell. We Americans have a soft spot for cupcakes, after all.

BREAKING IT DOWN

In order to get the rich nutty flavor just right, it's important to cook the butter until it reaches a deep brown color and you can smell its rich, nutty flavor. Don't be alarmed—you actually *want* the butter to burn and turn brown. One of my testers (she's also one of my coworkers), Annie Smallwood, had a great tip: As the butter browns, it makes a crackling sound. Pay close attention, because as soon as the sound stops, the butter should be just about right.

I recommend using a chinois when straining the butter into the naked cupcake mixture to ensure that burnt bits never reach your batter.

It's best to let the batter sit overnight in the refrigerator before baking, but if this is a naked cupcake emergency, they'll still taste good if the batter is freshly made.

 # Naked Cupcakes

INGREDIENTS	QUANTITY
Confectioners' sugar	1¼ cups
Almond flour	½ cup
All-purpose flour	¼ cup
Cocoa powder	2 tablespoons
Salt	⅛ teaspoon
Egg whites, warmed to room temperature	4 large
Applesauce	1 tablespoon plus ¼ teaspoon
Unsalted butter, warmed to room temperature	1 stick plus 1 tablespoon (9 tablespoons)
Raspberries, fresh	6 ounces

Preheat the oven to 350°F.

1. Mix all the dry ingredients (the confectioners' sugar, almond flour, all-purpose flour, cocoa powder, and salt) together by hand and sift them into a mixing bowl.

2.. Add the egg whites and applesauce to the dry ingredient mixture. Mix well.

3. Heat the butter in a saucepan over medium-high heat until it has thoroughly browned (it should be light caramel in color with dark "burnt" specks).

4. Using a chinois or other fine mesh strainer, strain the browned butter into the batter. Use a hand whisk to mix until thoroughly combined.

5. Place the batter in the refrigerator and let it cool overnight.

6. Pour the batter into the greased cupcake pans, and place about 5 raspberries in the center of each cupcake.

7. Bake for 20 to 25 minutes at 350°F or until the edges of the cupcakes are firm (the center may remain a little "jiggly" because of the moisture in the raspberries).

8. Cool thoroughly on a wire rack. Store in an airtight box.

Based on the Chocolate Financier recipe from the French Pastry School

Kiss and make up with a little help from this soufflé

ACTIVE TIME 45 minutes

YIELD

5 (3-inch diameter) soufflés

PREP

Take your eggs and butter out of the refrigerator a couple of hours before you plan to prepare the soufflés.

Preheat the oven to 400°F.

Prepare the ramekins by coating them entirely with softened butter using a pastry brush. Then, pour a handful of granulated sugar into the ramekins. Invert the ramekins over the sink, shaking out any excess sugar.

INGREDIENT FINDER

Bread flour is different from all-purpose flour. You can read more about the different types of flour on page 22.

Vanilla bean paste is available at Sur La Table and other fine culinary stores. I really love Nielsen-Massey's vanilla bean paste. You can find it online at Pastry Chef Central.

GRAB THESE

Sifter

Stand mixer fitted with the paddle attachment or a hand mixer

Pastry brush

Whisk

Ramekins for the individual soufflés

SHELF LIFE AND STORAGE INSTRUCTIONS

Unfortunately, the shelf life for these delicious delights is just 10 short minutes. Soufflés must be eaten immediately, as the egg whites start to deflate and the soufflé begins to fall almost immediately after it is removed from the oven.

Did your jealous side rear its ugly head? Trying to make amends? Timing is everything with these **chocolate soufflés**, so make sure that the make-up session occurs *after* this blissful treat comes out of the oven. This recipe is from my alma mater, the French Pastry School.

BREAKING IT DOWN

This is a great recipe to make for your beau, but it's not so great for a big dinner party, because it requires a lot of last-minute preparation. If you really want to wow a bunch of your friends the next time you entertain, you can make the base ahead of time and then whip and fold in your egg-white mixture *à la minute* (that's French for "at the last minute").

If you're making this recipe just for two, you should cut the recipe in half; this recipe will make 5 individual soufflés.

The consistency of the egg whites in this recipe is crucial. If the whites are overmixed, your soufflé will probably crack. But if don't whip your whites enough, they'll lack strength, and your soufflé won't rise. Also, don't get impatient and open the oven door. Soufflés are quite finicky, and a drop in the oven temperature could ruin a perfectly good soufflé.

The sugar in the ramekins will caramelize during baking and give a crispy outside texture to the soufflés.

Sinful Chocolate Soufflés

PREPARING THE SOUFFLÉ BASE:

INGREDIENTS	QUANTITY
Unsalted butter, warmed to room temperature	3½ tablespoons
Granulated sugar	¾ cup
Bread flour, sifted	⅓ cup

1. Sift the bread flour.

2. In the bowl of a stand mixer fitted with the paddle attachment, or in a mixing bowl (if using a hand mixer), mix together the butter and sugar.

3. Add in the sifted flour, stirring until it is barely mixed together. The mixture should have a coarse, clumpy appearance. Transfer this mixture to a clean mixing bowl and set aside.

PREPARING THE SOUFFLÉS:

INGREDIENTS	QUANTITY
Unsalted butter, warmed to room temperature	1½ teaspoons
Granulated sugar, for sprinkling	¼ cup (roughly)
Whole milk	¾ cup
Vanilla bean paste (or vanilla bean)	¾ teaspoon (or the seeds of ¼ of a vanilla bean, or ½ teaspoon vanilla extract)
Soufflé Base (see previous page)	1 recipe
Egg yolks, warmed to room temperature	2 large
Granulated sugar	¼ cup
Corn starch	1 tablespoon
Cocoa powder	1 tablespoon plus 1½ teaspoons
Egg whites, warmed to room temperature	4 large
Salt	⅛ teaspoon

Preheat the oven to 400°F.

1. Using a pastry brush, line the ramekins with softened butter and then sprinkle them with the ¼ cup granulated sugar for sprinkling. Pour out any excess sugar that doesn't stick to the butter.

2. In a saucepan, bring the milk and vanilla paste to a boil. Add the soufflé base to the pan, and whisk the mixture together rapidly for about 20 seconds.

3. Remove the mixture from heat and transfer to a medium mixing bowl.

4. Gently stir in the egg yolks. Cover the mixture with plastic wrap and set aside.

5. Combine the remaining granulated sugar, corn starch, and cocoa powder.

6. In a clean mixing bowl, whip the egg whites and salt together until the mixture forms stiff peaks. Fold* the granulated sugar–cocoa powder mixture into the whipped egg whites. Then, fold the soufflé mixture into the combined egg white–cocoa powder mixture.

7. Pour the mixture into the ramekins until each is ¾ of the way full. Bake at 400°F for about 15 minutes, and the soufflés have risen high beyond the ramekins' rims.

* Folding is the process of incorporating two different ingredients by gently "folding" part of the mixture into the other part. Start in the center of the mixture and lift the batter up and over itself, turning the bowl as you continue.

Based on the Classic French Soufflé recipe from the French Pastry School

Day-to-Day Happenings

You don't need a special occasion to make out-of-this-world baked goods! In fact, there are several everyday situations in life that can be made much merrier with the right baked goods. Whether you are dreading the awful airplane food on tomorrow's trip or looking for the perfect breakfast-on-the-go treat, this chapter will improve your life with a few terrific recipes.

- **Banana–Chocolate Chip Pound Cake**
- **Mom's Granola**
- **French Pistachio Macarons**
- **Rafael's Pistachio Buttercream Filling**
- **Bittersweet Chocolate Chip Cookies**

Make the journey home a lot more fun—and delicious

ACTIVE TIME 30 minutes

YIELD 1 (9 × 5 × 3) loaf

PREP

Take your eggs and butter out of the refrigerator a couple of hours before you plan to prepare the batter.

Preheat the oven to 350°F.

Prepare a 9 × 5 × 3 loaf pan by coating it entirely with softened butter using a pastry brush. Then, pour a handful of flour into the pan. Invert the pan over the sink, shaking out any excess flour.

INGREDIENT FINDER

I prefer bittersweet chocolate with a 60–70% cocoa content (64% is my favorite), but if you like milk chocolate, feel free to use it instead!

Mascarpone cheese can be found in the cheese section of most supermarkets and specialty food stores, including Whole Foods.

GRAB THESE

Sifter

Four mixing bowls

Stand mixer fitted with the paddle attachment or hand mixer

SHELF LIFE AND STORAGE INSTRUCTIONS

2 to 3 days stored at room temperature. Best if enjoyed within 1 to 2 days.

Are you heading home for the holidays and trying to mentally prepare yourself for the headache with the amiable name "traveling"? Unfortunately, I can't help you with the security lines and the carry-on guidelines. My dad instilled in me early on that Levys *do not* check their baggage, so imagine my shock the first time around as I watched $50 worth of hair products and sunblock get confiscated!

Clearly, you shouldn't take my advice about packing your luggage, but you can take my advice about what to cook up for the airplane ride. Bake a loaf of **banana–chocolate chip pound cake** the night before, and it will still be perfectly fresh and tasty for the plane ride. You may want to bake an extra loaf for the flight attendants (they're the right people to have on your side).

BREAKING IT DOWN

The key to delicious and moist banana cake is making sure you have extremely ripe bananas —nice and dirty-brown. Trying to make tasty banana bread with pale green bananas is like trying to make your eyelashes look voluptuous with old, clumpy mascara! Ideally, buy the bananas ahead of time and store them in a brown bag in a drawer; do not refrigerate them. If you're making this for a plane ride, presumably you have booked your tickets in advance and can plan ahead with the bananas! Helpful hint: If you are in a pinch, I suggest begging a produce department employee to find some ripe bananas in the back (they usually pull the bananas that look too ripe and throw them away).

Banana-Chocolate Chip Pound Cake

INGREDIENTS	QUANTITY
Mini bittersweet chocolate chips	½ cup
All-purpose flour	1⅛ cups
Baking powder	1½ teaspoons
Baking soda	1½ teaspoons
Salt	⅛ teaspoon
Sour cream	¼ cup
Mascarpone cheese, warmed to room temperature	¼ cup
Unsalted butter, warmed to room temperature	6 tablespoons (¾ stick)
Cinnamon, ground	¼ teaspoon
Granulated sugar	½ cup
Whole eggs, warmed to room temperature	1 large
Bananas, ripe, puréed	1 large (½ cup)

Preheat the oven to 350°F.

1. Mix a handful of flour into the chocolate chips to coat them (this ensures that the chocolate chips don't all end up at the bottom of the loaf).

2. Sift together the flour, baking powder, baking soda, and salt.

3. Combine the sour cream and mascarpone cheese in a bowl with a spatula.

4. In the bowl of a stand mixer fitted with the paddle attachment, or in a mixing bowl (if using a hand mixer), cream together the butter and cinnamon on high speed (you can always do it by hand, too). Gradually add in the sugar, about 1 tablespoon at a time. Continue to beat until the mixture is light in color and fluffy in texture.

5. Stop the mixer and scrape down the sides of the bowl. Then, turn the mixer back on to medium speed and add in the egg. (The mixer should remain running on medium speed through step 8.)

6. Add ⅓ of the flour mixture to the mixing bowl, beating until just incorporated.

7. Add ⅓ of the sour cream–mascarpone mixture to the mixing bowl until it is just barely incorporated.

8. Alternate adding in the rest of the flour and sour cream–mascarpone mixtures to the mixing bowl.

9. Turn off the mixer. Using a spatula, fold* in the puréed bananas and the miniature chocolate chips. Do not overmix.

10. Bake at 350°F for 50 minutes, or until a toothpick inserted into the center of the pound cake comes out clean.

* *Folding* is the process of incorporating two different ingredients by gently folding part of the mixture into the other part. Start in the center of the mixture and lift the batter up and over itself, turning the bowl as you continue.

Helpful hint: You can purée your bananas in a food processor if you have one, or you can "mash" them by hand using a spatula or wooden spoon.

Even a breakfast on the go can be sweet and delicious

ACTIVE TIME
30 minutes

YIELD
About 7 cups

PREP
Preheat the oven to 350°F.

INGREDIENT FINDER
Shredded sweetened coconut and wheat germ can be found at any supermarket.

GRAB THESE
2 baking sheets

Small saucepan (to melt the butter and honey)

SHELF LIFE AND STORAGE INSTRUCTIONS
14 days stored in an airtight container or ziplock bag at room temperature

I wish I could say I have fond childhood memories of my mom slaving away in the kitchen. In fact, she's more the ordering-in or going-out-to-eat type. But when she *does* whip up something in the kitchen, it's always delicious. Unlike her fudge recipe, which my dad claims she's made well only once in her life, she always executes her **granola** recipe perfectly. So if you consider yourself more of a novice in the kitchen, this recipe is for you. It's nearly impossible to screw up!

My mom's granola recipe is so tasty you don't even need milk with it. Take along a ziplock bag full of it to work to brighten your day with a snack, or try topping some yogurt with it. Add a few berries, and you've got a well-balanced breakfast.

BREAKING IT DOWN

Granola is such a great item to have on hand. It has a two-week shelf life, so it's a pretty low-maintenance treat. I'm sure you have family recipes that bring back memories, too. This granola will always remind me of my mom, which is why I love making it and sharing it with friends (well, nowadays, Chef Rafael makes it—and his version is *amazing*!).

If you allow the granola to cool completely before storing it, clumps will form. Who doesn't love eating a giant clump of granola?

*Helpful Hint: The better the butter, the better the granola. I recommend the richest and most indulgent butter on the market, Plugra. You can find it at most better supermarkets.

 # Mom's Granola

INGREDIENTS	QUANTITY
Quaker instant oats	4 cups
Wheat germ	½ cup
Shredded sweetened coconut	1 cup
Raisins	1½ cups
Unsalted butter, warmed to room temperature	2 sticks (16 tablespoons)
Honey	¾ cup

Preheat the oven to 350°F.

1. In a mixing bowl, combine all the dry ingredients.

2. Heat the butter and honey in a saucepan over medium heat. Bring to a boil for 1 minute.

3. Pour the hot butter–honey mixture over the dry ingredients, stirring until it is fully incorporated.

4. Spread the mixture on baking sheets and bake at 350°F for about 30 to 45 minutes or until golden brown, stirring every 10 minutes or so.

5. Let the granola cool completely before transferring it to an airtight container or ziplock bags.

Having a bad day? Need an indulgent treat?

ACTIVE TIME 1½ hours

YIELD About 40 (80 halves)

PREP

Take your eggs out of the refrigerator a couple of hours before you plan to prepare the macarons.

Preheat the oven to 325°F.

Assemble a pastry bag with a #804 or #16 tip (see page 20).

Line 2 baking sheets with parchment paper.

INGREDIENT FINDER

Instead of light corn syrup, I use glucose syrup for this recipe at my shop. Glucose syrup is a gooey type of sugar that has 50% sweetening power (granulated sugar has 100% sweetening power). Its texture is similar to that of light corn syrup, which is why corn syrup is a perfectly acceptable alternative to use here. It can be very hard to find (you can find both glucose syrup and almond flour online at Pastry Chef Central), but if you want to be really true to the original, go for it! Learn more about glucose syrup on page 26.

Almond flour is simply ground-up almonds. Read more about it on page 23.

Green food coloring is available at Sur La Table and most supermarkets. I prefer the Chefmaster and Americolor brands.

GRAB THESE

Sifter

Stand mixer fitted with the whisk attachment or hand mixer

Candy thermometer

2 pastry bags fitted with a coupler and a round tip (#804 or #16) (you can use the same tip for both applications)

Parchment paper

2 baking sheets

Rubber spatula

Offset spatula

SHELF LIFE AND STORAGE INSTRUCTIONS

You can store them in the refrigerator for 7 days, or in the freezer for up to 6 months.

This recipe for **French Pistachio Macarons** is truly decadent, and the best part is that they freeze beautifully. You can make these when you have some spare time and stow them in the freezer for when you need a pick-me-up on a rotten day.

Don't be intimidated by the fact that the humidity level in your kitchen will determine whether this recipe will turn out just right or end up looking like a seven-year-old made it. When they do turn out just right, with a light and crisp shell around a soft center filled with pistachio buttercream, you'll realize that it was well worth the hassle (just like most of the good things in life).

Ladies, as you know, it's all about confidence. If that doesn't do the trick, you can always order these from my shop and pretend they're homemade. I'll never tell.

BREAKING IT DOWN

One tip for creating flawless macarons is to let the macarons sit on the baking sheet for a half-hour before putting them in the oven. If you do, a "shell" will form that helps prevent the macarons from cracking.

This recipe calls for egg whites, but be sure you save the yolks as you prepare it—you'll be filling the macarons with Rafael's Pistachio Buttercream Filling (see page 96), which requires egg yolks!

French Pistachio Macarons

INGREDIENTS	QUANTITY
Mixture A:	
Confectioners' sugar	1¾ cups
Almond flour	2 cups
Egg whites	2 large (¼ cup)
Mixture B:	
Granulated sugar	¾ cup plus 2 tablespoons
Water	¼ cup
Light corn syrup	2 teaspoons
Egg whites, warmed to room temperature	3 large (⅓ cup)
Salt	Pinch (1/16 teaspoon)
Green food coloring	As needed
Rafael's Pistachio Buttercream Filling (see page 96)	1 recipe

Preheat the oven to 325°F.

Mixture A:

1. Sift the confectioners' sugar into a mixing bowl. Sift the almond flour into the same bowl.

2. Mix in the 2 raw (not whipped) egg whites with a rubber spatula.

Mixture B:

1. In a medium saucepan, heat the granulated sugar, water, and corn syrup to 248°F over medium heat.

2. As the granulated sugar, water, and corn syrup mixture is heating, start to lightly beat together the 3 egg whites and salt in a separate bowl until light and frothy.

3. Once the sugar syrup mixture reaches 248°F, turn the mixer to high speed and slowly pour the sugar syrup into the beaten egg whites. Beat the mixture until it forms stiff peaks, about 5 to 6 minutes, creating a meringue that appears shiny and stiff (similar to shaving cream).

4. Add a few drops of the green food coloring and mix until thoroughly combined and the desired color is achieved.

Putting it all together:

5. Fold Mixture B into Mixture A in three separate additions. To test whether the consistency is correct and you have sufficiently folded together the ingredients, plop a dollop of the mixture onto a hard surface with your finger. At first, a little "tip" should be visible. If the tip disappears, leaving a flat, smooth surface, you've got the perfect consistency.

6. Fill the piping bag halfway with the macaron mixture.

7. Pipe round circles, about 1 inch in diameter, onto parchment paper–lined baking sheets (leaving about 1½ inches of space between each). Try counting to three as you pipe each one in order to make them consistent in size.

8. Let the macarons sit at room temperature for 30 minutes before placing them in the oven.

9. Bake at 325°F for 10 to 12 minutes. The top should be slightly "crisp" and the center nice and soft.

10. Once the macarons have cooled completely, remove them from the baking sheets using an offset spatula. Place them on sheets of parchment paper in 20 groups of 2 each. Using a clean piping bag fitted with a round #804 tip, place a small dollop of Rafael's Pistachio Buttercream Filling on one side of each of the macarons in the first group. Next, attach a single macaron from the second group to the each of the macarons in the first group, making each into a pistachio buttercream sandwich.

11. Store the finished macarons in an airtight container in the refrigerator.

Based on the Macarons recipe from the French Pastry School.

Something scrumptious to fill up those macarons

ACTIVE TIME
40 minutes

YIELD
Filling for 40 French macarons
(4 cups)

PREP
Take your butter and eggs out of the refrigerator a couple of hours before you plan to prepare the filling.

INGREDIENT FINDER
Pistachio paste can be found online at Amazon, Pastry Chef Central, and King Arthur Flour. If you don't want to wait, you can always make pistachio paste yourself. Do a Google search for "pistachio paste recipe," and make it yourself *just like that*!

GRAB THESE
Spatula

Stand mixer fitted with the whisk attachment and/or a hand mixer

Candy thermometer

SHELF LIFE AND STORAGE INSTRUCTIONS
Store in the refrigerator for 7 days, or in the freezer for up to 6 months.

Rafael's Pistachio Buttercream Filling is another amazing recipe straight from the talented mind of Chef Rafael Ornelas. You can use this same recipe to make any nut-flavored buttercream, such as hazelnut or peanut butter. Pistachio buttercream adds an element of richness to this otherwise "light" dessert. Leave it to an American to add fat to an otherwise health*ier* French pastry.

BREAKING IT DOWN

The yolks in this buttercream recipe help make it extra creamy and rich. In order to ensure that the pistachio paste blends into the buttercream well, first add scoopfuls of the buttercream mixture (the yolks and sugar syrup) into the pistachio paste/butter mixture. Doing so will change the thick paste into a creamier mixture, which will help it blend well with the buttercream. Who wants to be stuck with lumpy pistachio buttercream?

 # Rafael's Pistachio Buttercream Filling

INGREDIENTS	QUANTITY
Pistachio paste	⅓ cup
Unsalted butter, warmed to room temperature	4 sticks (32 tablespoons)
Egg yolks, warmed to room temperature	5 large
Granulated sugar	¾ cup
Water	¼ cup

1. In a small mixing bowl, mix together the pistachio paste and butter either by hand with a rubber spatula or with a hand mixer.

2. In the bowl of a stand mixer fitted with the whisk attachment, or in a separate mixing bowl (if using a hand mixer), whip the yolks on high speed until they are very pale in color and have doubled in volume (about 4 to 5 minutes).

3. In a small saucepan on medium heat, heat the sugar and water together. The temperature of the mixture should reach 235 to 240°F (that's the "soft ball" stage; for more on that, see page 75).

4. With the mixer running on high speed, gradually add the hot sugar syrup to the yolks, which should look pale, fluffy, and voluminous. Once the syrup has been added in its entirety, decrease the speed to low and beat until the mixture has thoroughly cooled (about 5 minutes).

5. For best results, before adding the butter–pistachio paste to the mixture, add a few scoopfuls of the yolk–syrup mixture and mix it in well. The objective is to make the two mixtures' consistency more alike, which will create a smoother mixture. Then, add in the rest of butter–pistachio paste mixture and mix thoroughly.

6. Use the filling as directed in the French Pistachio Macarons recipe (see page 94).

If you pack these to snack on in traffic ...

ACTIVE TIME 30 minutes

YIELD About 48 cookies

PREP

Take your eggs and butter out of the refrigerator a couple of hours before you make the cookie dough.

Preheat the oven to 350°F.

Line the baking sheets with parchment paper.

Sift the flour.

INGREDIENT FINDER

Quality is important when it comes to vanilla extract and butter. I recommend Nielsen-Massey brand vanilla, which is available at Williams-Sonoma stores nationwide and online. You can find Plugra butter at most better supermarkets.

GRAB THESE

Sifter

Stand mixer fitted with the paddle attachment or a hand mixer

Parchment paper

2 baking sheets

Cookie scoop

Wire rack

SHELF LIFE AND STORAGE INSTRUCTIONS

The dough will stay fresh for 4 to 5 days in the refrigerator and for up to 6 months in the freezer.

The baked cookies will stay fresh for 2 days, stored in an airtight container.

You may intentionally schedule your departure times around the busiest rush hour! They are the perfect treat to de-stress at the end of the day. I love eating these soft, yet crisp **bittersweet chocolate chip cookies** with a glass of milk; if I really want to indulge, I dip them into a cup of hot chocolate. The center of each cookie is soft, and the edges have a little bit of crispness.

BREAKING IT DOWN

The cookie will be as good as the chocolate you use to make them, so I recommend purchasing a couverture 64% cocoa paste chocolate (see page 24 for details). Vahlrona, Cocoa Barry, Felchlin, and Dagoba are all great brands.

Here's a great tip: This dough freezes beautifully. When you're planning to make these cookies, prepare more cookie dough than you'll need, shape the excess into balls using a cookie or ice cream scoop, and drop each of the extra balls into a gallon-size ziplock freezer bag. If you don't have a cookie or ice cream scoop, you can use a spoon to place dollops of dough onto the baking sheet. They just won't be as perfectly round as the scooped cookies.

 # Bittersweet Chocolate Chip Cookies

INGREDIENTS	QUANTITY
Unsalted butter, warmed to room temperature	2½ sticks (20 tablespoons)
Granulated sugar	½ cup
Light brown sugar	1 cup
Vanilla extract	3 teaspoons
Whole eggs, warmed to room temperature	2 large
Salt	¾ teaspoon
All-purpose flour, sifted	2¼ cup
Baking soda	1 teaspoon
Bittersweet chocolate chips	2 cups (12 ounces)
Pecans, chopped	2 cups

Preheat the oven to 350°F.

1. In the bowl of a stand mixer fitted with the paddle attachment, or in a mixing bowl (if using a hand mixer), cream together the butter, sugars (white and brown), and vanilla extract on medium speed until well combined, about 1 minute.

2. As the mixer continues to run, add the eggs, one at a time, until they are incorporated into the mixture.

3. Reduce the speed of the mixer to low and slowly mix in the salt, flour, and baking soda until just combined.

4. Add the chocolate chips and nuts to the cookie dough mixture.

5. Using a 2-inch cookie or ice cream scoop, scoop the dough into balls and place them on the prepared baking sheets.

6. Bake at 350°F for 10 to 12 minutes, or until the edges are golden brown. Cool on a wire rack.

Hostess Gifts

While your presence alone is enough for some hostesses, a present (especially a home-baked one) will never go unappreciated. Show up to the next party you're invited to with one of these wonderful goodies, and every guest at the party will want to invite you to their next party.

- **Decadent Chocolate–Almond Toffee**
- **Raspberry Pepin Jam**
- **Rafael's Toffee Sugar Cookies**
- **Vanilla Bean Chocolate Truffles**
- **Lemon Baby Rattle Cookies**

Make your dinner party hostess love you forever!

ACTIVE TIME 1½ hours

YIELD 3¼ pounds

PREP

Preheat the oven to 350°F and toast your 2 pounds of slivered almonds by roasting them on a dry baking sheet at 350°F for 15 minutes, or until golden brown.

Make the toffee centers at least the day before you plan to finish the recipe to ensure that the toffee has cooled completely before dipping it in chocolate. If you're in a rush, you can always pop the centers in the freezer for 20 to 30 minutes before dipping.

Line 3 baking sheets with parchment paper.

INGREDIENT FINDER

Instead of light corn syrup, I use glucose syrup for this recipe at my shop. Glucose syrup is a gooey type of sugar that has 50% sweetening power (granulated sugar has 100% sweetening power). Its texture is similar to that of light corn syrup, which is why corn syrup is a perfectly acceptable alternative to use here. It can be very hard to find (you can find it online at Pastry Chef Central), but if you want to be really true to the original, go for it! Learn more about glucose syrup on page 26.

GRAB THESE

Pyrex bowl (for melting chocolate)

2 baking sheets

Parchment paper

Candy thermometer

Whisk

Offset spatula

Latex gloves (for dipping the toffee in the chocolate)

Food processor (if you don't have one, you can chop the slivered almonds by hand with a chef's knife, use a spice grinder, or even use a mortar and pestle, if you have one)

SHELF LIFE AND STORAGE INSTRUCTIONS

1 month in an airtight container at room temperature. Don't refrigerate, because the condensation in the refrigerator will harm the texture of the toffee.

It doesn't matter who's making the dinner: No one in her right mind would turn down a box of handmade **chocolate–almond toffee**. This candy has a one-month shelf life, which is great news for your hostess: she can choose to either share it with her guests or selfishly save it for later. And remember—you can make it a gift that keeps on giving by writing the recipe on a note card and including it with the gift.

BREAKING IT DOWN

To ensure that the toffee is thoroughly cooked, place a tiny amount of it onto your countertop using a small offset spatula or spoon. Once it has completely cooled, take a bite. It should be crunchy, and it should not stick to your teeth.

If you want to save your nails from becoming embedded with chocolate, I suggest that you wear gloves during the dipping process.

The corn syrup in this recipe is critical because it helps prevent the sugar from crystallizing. That's necessary because you don't want lumpy sugar balls to form in your smooth, beautiful toffee.

Be sure to set aside and freeze some of this toffee to have it on hand when making **Rafael's toffee sugar cookies** (see page 108). Remove the desired amount of toffee from the batch before you dip it in the chocolate and almonds.

Decadent Chocolate– Almond Toffee

INGREDIENTS	QUANTITY
Unsalted butter, warmed to room temperature	3½ sticks (28 tablespoons)
Granulated sugar	2⅓ cups plus 2 tablespoons
Salt	½ teaspoon
Water	¼ cup
Light corn syrup	⅛ cup
Slivered almonds, toasted (see directions at left in the sidebar under Prep)	2 pounds, divided
Bittersweet chocolate	1 pound

1. Place the butter in a saucepan and melt it on low heat. Add the sugar, salt, water, and corn syrup, and cook on medium heat, stirring occasionally with a whisk, until the mixture reaches 260.6°F.

2. Add ⅛ of the almonds and cook until the mixture reaches 305°F. Remove from heat.

3. Using an offset spatula, remove the toffee from the saucepan and spread it on 2 of the lined baking sheets to cool.

4. Melt the chocolate in your microwave at 50% power for 3 to 5 minutes (in 1-minute increments, stirring well in between). The chocolate should reach 90°F when thoroughly melted.

HOW TO DIP THE TOFFEE IN THE MELTED CHOCOLATE:

1. Once the toffee has cooled completely, break it up into smaller pieces and place it in a bowl. To speed up the cooling process, you can place the toffee in the freezer for 15 to 30 minutes. (I don't recommend putting it in the refrigerator because of the condensation factor there.) It's up to you how big or small you would like your pieces to be. I personally like them to be on the smaller side, because you get a better chocolate-to-toffee ratio. Keep in mind that the pieces will get bigger once they are dipped in chocolate. Note: If you plan to use some of the cooled toffee to make Rafael's Toffee Sugar Cookies recipe (see page 108), set that amount of toffee aside now, because the toffee in the cookies should not be dipped in chocolate.

2. Reline the baking sheets you cooled the toffee on with parchment paper.

3. Grind or finely chop the remaining 1¾ pounds of toasted almonds with a knife. Spread them on 1 of the 3 lined baking sheets.

4. Using your left hand, pick up each piece of toffee and dip it into the chocolate. Wipe off the excess chocolate and place the piece of toffee on the tray containing the chopped almonds. Using your right (chocolate-free) hand, quickly cover the chocolate-covered toffee with the almonds.

5. Once the chocolate has set (after about 15 minutes), you can transfer the toffee pieces to the remaining lined baking sheet (feel free to pile them on top of each other). If the chocolate isn't set by 15 minutes, you can pop it into the refrigerator for 30 minutes.

Store in an airtight container at room temperature for up to 1 month. Do not refrigerate.

Brighten up any holiday party with jam

ACTIVE TIME
30 minutes

YIELD
1 quart

PREP
None needed! This one's awfully easy.

INGREDIENT FINDER
All ingredients can be found easily at any supermarket.

GRAB THIS
Candy thermometer

SHELF LIFE AND STORAGE INSTRUCTIONS
1 month stored in an airtight container in the refrigerator

Anybody can show up at a holiday party bearing a bottle of wine. But if you want to be the kind of guest who always gets invited back, show up with a jar of homemade **raspberry pepin jam** instead.

Jams are an everyday indulgence—sweet, cozy and comforting—but when they're made by a friend, they're really special. Just one jar will make your friends think of you the very next morning, as they literally spread holiday cheer on their toast. Of course, eventually the jar will be empty—and then your friends will have to invite you over again.

BREAKING IT DOWN

This recipe can be used with practically any kind of fruit, so feel free to substitute your favorite fruit for the raspberries. Keep in mind that sweeter fruits require less sugar.

It's always great to have homemade jam on hand because it can make a simple piece of toast taste extra special.

 # Raspberry Pepin Jam

INGREDIENTS	QUANTITY
Raspberries, fresh	7 cups (1 pound, 14 ounces)
Granulated sugar	4 cups, divided
Salt	¼ teaspoon
Lemon juice	3 tablespoons

1. In a saucepan over medium heat, combine the raspberries with the sugar. Bring the mixture to a boil.

2. As soon as the mixture reaches a boil, add the salt and continue cooking until the mixture reaches 220°F.

3. Turn off the heat, add the lemon juice, and stir until combined. That's it!

4. You can store the jam in a tightly sealed jar in the refrigerator for 1 month. For presentation purposes, I recommend using small, clear jars; you can decorate the jars by tying bright fabrics onto the lids.

Based on the Raspberry Pepin Jam recipe from the French Pastry School.

Your friend won't want to leave without these cookies

ANNA BLESSING

ACTIVE TIME

45 minutes if you have the Decadent Chocolate–Almond Toffee (see page 104) already prepared; 1½ hours if you have to make both the toffee and the cookies.

YIELD

24 cookies

PREP

Make the dough at least two hours before you're ready to bake the cookies and refrigerate it in the meantime.

Take your eggs and butter out of the refrigerator a couple of hours before you plan to prepare the cookie batter.

Make Decadent Chocolate–Almond Toffee.

After the dough has rested in the refrigerator for at least two hours, preheat the oven to 350°F.

Line the baking sheets with parchment paper.

Grind toffee pieces with a mortar and pestle, spice grinder, or food processor. You could also just use a chef's knife and cutting board.

INGREDIENT FINDER

You should be able to find all the ingredients easily at your local supermarket.

GRAB THESE

Stand mixer fitted with the paddle attachment or a hand mixer

2 baking sheets

Parchment paper

Wooden spoon

Cookie cutter(s)

Rolling pin

Marble slab (or just clean off the kitchen counter with water mixed with a few drops of bleach), for rolling out dough

Mortar and pestle, spice grinder, or food processor for grinding the toffee

Decadent Chocolate–Almond Toffee (see recipe on page 104)

SHELF LIFE AND STORAGE INSTRUCTIONS

1 week stored in an airtight container at room temperature. Dough can be refrigerated for up to 10 days and frozen for up to 6 months.

Send off your friend with your very best—a dozen **toffee sugar cookies**. This is Chef Rafael's recipe, and it was featured in *Chicago* magazine as one of the top 123 dishes to eat in Chicago. The story behind how this cookie recipe came to be is one of my favorites: a new cook made a batch of toffee that didn't turn out quite right. Chef Rafael didn't want to waste it, so he decided to grind it up into smaller pieces and use it in a sugar cookie recipe. Who knew that this would become one of our most popular items? Great things often come from mistakes.

To make these cookies taste even better, try dipping half of each cookie in chocolate. Refer to the **chocolate-covered strawberries** recipe (see page 54) for directions on melting and tempering the chocolate.

BREAKING IT DOWN

For best results, use our **decadent chocolate-almond toffee** recipe (see page 104), *sans* chocolate, for the toffee pieces. If you don't have any toffee pieces in the freezer, you can buy Heath bars and chop them up into small pieces.

If you're like me and sometimes just don't have the time or patience to let the dough rest, just use an ice cream scoop or spoon to place gobs of dough 2½ inches apart on the baking sheet and bypass the rolling and cutting stage altogether!

 # Rafael's Toffee Sugar Cookies

INGREDIENTS	QUANTITY
All-purpose flour	4 cups
Baking powder	¾ teaspoons
Salt	¾ teaspoons
Unsalted butter, warmed to room temperature	3 sticks (24 tablespoons)
Light brown sugar	1½ cups, packed
Whole eggs, warmed to room temperature	2 large
Vanilla extract	1½ teaspoons
Pieces of Decadent Chocolate–Almond Toffee (see page 104), ground into small chunks	1½ cups

Preheat the oven to 350°F.

1. In a small mixing bowl, mix together the flour, baking powder, and salt.

2. In the bowl of a stand mixer fitted with the paddle attachment, or in a mixing bowl (if using a hand mixer), cream together the butter and sugar until fluffy.

3. As the mixer continues to run, mix in the eggs and vanilla extract until combined.

4. In two batches, add the dry ingredient mixture to the wet ingredient mixture and mix until combined.

5. Shut off the mixer and stir the toffee pieces into the mixture by hand using a wooden spoon or rubber spatula.

6. Cover the dough with plastic wrap and refrigerate for 2 hours.

7. On a lightly floured work surface, roll out the dough using a rolling pin to a ½-inch thickness. (Make sure you sprinkle the top of the dough with flour before using the rolling pin on it.) Cut out the cookies with a square or round cookie cutter and place them 2 inches apart on the prepared baking sheets.

8. Bake at 350°F for about 20 minutes, or until golden brown.

Sweet little bites for a beautiful wedding shower

ACTIVE TIME 1 hour

YIELD 20 truffles

PREP

Make the ganache the night before, as it must cool overnight in the refrigerator.

Line 2 baking sheets with parchment paper.

INGREDIENT FINDER

Instead of light corn syrup, I use glucose syrup for this recipe at my shop. Glucose syrup is a gooey type of sugar that has 50% sweetening power (granulated sugar has 100% sweetening power). Its texture is similar to that of light corn syrup, which is why corn syrup is a perfectly acceptable alternative to use here. It can be very hard to find (you can find it online at Pastry Chef Central), but if you want to be really true to the original, go for it! Learn more about glucose syrup on page 26.

See information on varieties of chocolate on pages 23 and 24.

I prefer Cocoa Barry cocoa powder, which you can find at Whole Foods and other quality stores. Use your leftover powder to make amazing hot chocolate (the recipe is on the box).

GRAB THESE

2 baking sheets

Parchment paper

Candy thermometer

Offset spatula

Latex gloves, for dipping

1-inch ice cream scoop with a spring release

SHELF LIFE AND STORAGE INSTRUCTIONS

Store in a cool, dry place at room temperature for 3 to 4 days or in the refrigerator for 7 days.

The bride-to-be may be on a diet getting ready for the Big Day, but a few tiny **vanilla bean chocolate truffles** won't do too much damage. Chocolate truffles are a type of *ganache*, which is a combination of chocolate and cream (and what could be bad about that?).

Chocolate truffles were named for their fungi lookalike, the truffle. These forest-grown truffles are quite pricey, with some types fetching as much as $2,700 per pound. Their chocolate counterparts aren't quite that costly, but they add up quickly—many cost as much as $3 apiece. After you take the time to make them yourself, you'll understand why.

BREAKING IT DOWN

Do not overmix the ganache, or it will "break" and will not be smooth and creamy.

The photograph on page 112 shows the truffles I sell in my shop, which are tempered. Because you are coating the chocolate-dipped truffles with cocoa powder, you don't have to go through the tempering process, but you should still melt the chocolate gradually so it remains as close to 98°F as possible. You might want to try my earlier tip about using a heating pad to keep the chocolate warm as you do the dipping (see page 53). If the chocolate is too hot, it will be too thin and won't form a thick enough layer on the truffles. If it's too cold, it will be too thick and hard to work with.

 # Vanilla Bean Chocolate Truffles

INGREDIENTS	QUANTITY
For Ganache:	
Vanilla bean	½
Bittersweet chocolate (64%)	3 ounces
Milk chocolate (38%)	3 ounces
Heavy whipping cream	½ cup
Light corn syrup	1 tablespoon plus 1½ teaspoons
Unsalted butter, warmed to room temperature	1 tablespoon
For Coating:	
Chocolate (I like 64%), melted	1 pound
Cocoa powder	1 cup

1. Using a paring knife, extract the seeds from the vanilla bean by splitting the seed pod in half; then, rake the back side of the knife down the inside of the pod to scrape out the seeds.

2. In a mixing bowl, melt the dark and milk chocolate for the ganache halfway by heating it in the microwave for about 2 minutes at 50% power. By halfway, I mean that half of the chocolate should be melted, and the other half will still be solid. I like using chocolate pistoles or coins, but you can also just chop solid chocolate into small pieces before melting it. You may also use the double boiler method if you prefer (see page 17).

3. In a saucepan, combine the cream, vanilla bean seeds, and corn syrup, and bring the mixture to a boil. Remove the mixture from the heat.

4. Pour the hot cream mixture over the partially melted chocolate. Cover the bowl with plastic wrap and set aside for 5 minutes.

5. Using a rubber spatula, stir the cream–chocolate mixture in concentric circles, starting in the center of the bowl, only widening your stirring circle when the small area you are working through is thoroughly incorporated (it will look shiny and smooth). Always stir in the same direction to avoid "breaking" the ganache. Continue until the mixture is combined, creating a ganache.

6. Once the mixture cools to 100.4°F, mix in the room-temperature butter, stirring until thoroughly mixed.

7. Cool the mixture in the refrigerator overnight.

8. After the ganache has thoroughly cooled, use a 1-inch ice cream scoop (one with a spring release) to scoop out the ganache. After you create each scoop, roll it into a perfect ball in the palm of your hand. Place each ball at least 1 inch apart on one of your lined baking sheets.

9. Chop the coating chocolate into small chunks. Gradually warm the chocolate in the microwave at 50% power until it is completely melted (about 2 minutes). The chocolate is ready when it has reached 86°F.

10. Pour the cocoa powder into a small bowl.

11. Set up your *mise en place* (that's chef-speak for getting everything in place) by setting your ganache ball tray on your left, the bowl of melted chocolate and the bowl containing the cocoa powder in the center, and the other baking sheet lined with parchment paper on your right.

12. Using your left hand, drop each ganache ball first into the bowl of melted chocolate. Then, shake off excess chocolate and drop into the bowl of cocoa powder. Use your clean right hand to cover the truffle with cocoa powder and place on a parchment-lined baking sheet.

13. Repeat with each ganache ball, transferring the truffles onto the prepared baking sheet.

14. Before serving the truffles, allow them to gradually warm to room temperature (should take about 30 minutes). Ideally, truffles should be stored in a room that is approximately 65°F, but you can also store them at room temperature for 3 to 4 days or in the refrigerator for 1 week.

This recipe is a variation of the Rum Truffle recipe from my alma mater, the French Pastry School.

Oh, baby! What a beautiful little cookie!

ACTIVE TIME 1½ hours

YIELD 24 cookies

PREP

Take your eggs and butter out of the refrigerator a couple of hours before you make the dough.

Sift the confectioners' sugar and the flour.

Preheat the oven to 350°F.

Line 2 baking sheets with parchment paper.

INGREDIENT FINDER

The website Copper Gifts (www. coppergifts.com) offers a wide variety of cookie cutters; Sur La Table also has a great selection. Consider paying a visit to a craft store, like Michaels; many craft stores have extensive baking sections with lots of different cookie cutters.

GRAB THESE

Sifter

Rattle-shaped cookie cutters

Paring knife

Parchment paper

2 baking sheets lined with parchment paper

Marble slab (or just clean off the kitchen counter with water mixed with a few drops of bleach), for rolling out dough

Rolling pin

Stand mixer fitted with the paddle attachment or a hand mixer

SHELF LIFE AND STORAGE INSTRUCTIONS

7 days at room temperature in a sealed airtight container; dough can be stored for as long as 3 months in the freezer (see page 45 for instructions)

Take some weight off your pregnant friend's shoulders (after all, she's carrying around enough weight right there in her belly) by offering to make some delicious **lemon baby rattle cookies** for her shower. These cookies can be arranged as a centerpiece on each table, or can be placed at each person's seat as a favor.

These lemon cookies taste as delicious as they look. You can have fun with the design, and use any colors you wish for the icing.

BREAKING IT DOWN

The consistency of the icing for this recipe can be easily altered: You can thicken it by adding sifted confectioners' sugar or thin it by adding room-temperature water to the mixture. If you plan to dip the cookies in the icing, it should be slightly thinner, and if you plan to decorate them with a piping bag (especially if you plan to write with the icing), it should be thicker.

Chef Rafael Ornelas figured out that when making the icing, using a stand mixer's paddle attachment works much better than using the whisk attachment because it incorporates less air, and thus fewer air bubbles. (You can always use a hand mixer instead.) Also, make sure to strain the lemon juice so none of the seeds get into the icing.

Lemon Baby Rattle Cookies

INGREDIENTS	QUANTITY
Vanilla bean	1
Unsalted butter, warmed to room temperature	3 sticks plus 5 tablespoons (29 tablespoons)
Salt	¼ teaspoon
Lemon zest	2 lemons
Confectioners' sugar, sifted	1¾ cups
Egg yolks, warmed to room temperature (save the whites for the Royal Icing!)	2 large
All-purpose flour, sifted	3¾ cups
Royal Icing (see recipe on page 48)	1 recipe

Preheat the oven to 350°F.

1. Extract the vanilla bean seeds from each bean pod: Using a paring knife, split the bean in half, and use the blunt side of the knife to scrape out the seeds. Set the seeds aside and discard the pods, or stick them in a jar of sugar to make vanilla sugar.

2. In the bowl of a stand mixer fitted with the paddle attachment, or in a mixing bowl (if using a hand mixer), cream together the butter, salt, vanilla bean seeds, and lemon zest.

3. As the mixer continues to run, add in the confectioners' sugar, mixing thoroughly. Then, slowly add in the egg yolks, 1 at a time.

4. Stop the mixer, scrape the bowl, and turn the mixer back on. Then, slowly add in the sifted flour, ½ to ¼ cup at a time, until just combined (and you can't see any traces of the flour).

5. Cover the dough and refrigerate for at least 1 hour.

6. Remove the dough from the bowl. Lightly flour your work surface, and using a rolling pin, roll the dough into a disk about ½-inch thick. With your cookie cutters, cut out the cookies and place them 2 inches apart on the prepared baking sheets. Continue until you have used all the dough. If the dough becomes too soft, you may need to refrigerate it again for a bit.

7. Bake at 350°F for 12 minutes.

8. Let the cookies cool on a rack for 20 minutes (if you are in a rush, you can pop them in the refrigerator for about 10 minutes).

9. Decorate the cookies with Royal Icing (see recipe and instructions on page 48).

The holidays

Are you tired of bringing the same old-fashioned dessert to holiday gatherings every year? Try these fun twists on classic holiday desserts—I've got everything from a sour cherry pie engineered to cap off the Christmas dinner of your dreams to delicious coconut–apricot macaroons perfect for any Passover seder. Whatever your background may be, these recipes cross cultural boundaries and make everyone happy, and what more can you ask for during the holidays?

- **Rafael's Coconut–Apricot Macaroons**
- **Chocolate Molten Cakes**
- **Sour Cherry Pie**
- **Chocolate–Raspberry Brioche**
- **Uncle Page's Popovers**

Bring a round of smiles to the Passover seder table

ACTIVE TIME
30 minutes

YIELD
24 2-inch macaroons

PREP
Preheat the oven to 350°F.

Line 2 baking sheets with parchment paper.

INGREDIENT FINDER
Unsweetened coconut is available at Whole Foods Markets and Trader Joe's, or your local health food store. If you can't find unsweetened coconut, simply reduce the amount of sugar in the recipe by 2 tablespoons.

Make sure you buy *light* corn syrup, and not "lite" corn syrup. There's a big difference.

GRAB THESE
Cookie or ice cream scoop (1½-inch diameter)

2 baking sheets

Rubber spatula

Chef's knife

Cutting board

Parchment paper

SHELF LIFE AND STORAGE INSTRUCTIONS
Up to 4 days stored in an airtight container at room temperature.

Throughout history, Jews have had to *pass* on some great treats during Passover, but not any more! This recipe for **Rafael's coconut–apricot macaroons** is so good, you'll never miss the gluten.

BREAKING IT DOWN

You can easily alter this recipe, customizing it to your own tastes. You can spice up the traditional recipe by adding dried apricots, chocolate chips, dried cherries, or toffee pieces, for example. You might also consider dipping the macaroons in chocolate for a particularly luxurious treat.

To speed up the boiling process in the second step, use hot instead of room temperature water.

Rafael's Coconut–Apricot Macaroons

INGREDIENTS	QUANTITY
Dried apricots	1 cup
Unsweetened coconut	2½ cups
Water	3 tablespoons
Granulated sugar	¾ cup
Light corn syrup	1 tablespoon
Vanilla extract	2 teaspoons
Egg whites	2 large

Preheat the oven to 350°F.

1. Using your chef's knife, cut the dried apricots into small pieces, about ½ inch thick.

2. Place the coconut and apricot pieces in a mixing bowl. Set aside.

3. Combine the water, granulated sugar, and corn syrup in a saucepan and bring the mixture to a boil.

4. Pour the boiling water–sugar mixture into the bowl containing the coconut and apricot. Add the vanilla, stirring thoroughly.

5. Stir the egg whites into the mixture until combined. The mixture will have a thick consistency.

6. Using the cookie scoop, place small mounds of the mixture onto the prepared baking sheets, about 1 inch apart.

7. Bake at 350°F for 15 minutes, or until the tops and bottoms of the macaroons are lightly browned.

A Valentine's Day delight to share with your beloved

ACTIVE TIME 30 minutes

YIELD 8 cakes

PREP

Preheat the oven to 400°F.

Take your eggs and butter out of the refrigerator a couple of hours before you make the cakes.

INGREDIENT FINDER

You can find bittersweet chocolate almost anywhere, but I really love Valrhona chocolate, which is available at Trader Joe's stores.

GRAB THESE

Sifter

Double boiler (or just use your microwave—see page 17 for details)

Whisk

Stand mixer fitted with the whisk attachment or a hand mixer

8 ceramic ramekins (or 2 cupcake pans if you don't have ramekins)

SHELF LIFE AND STORAGE INSTRUCTIONS

The cakes can be refrigerated for 2 to 3 days and then reheated (either in the oven or the microwave) when needed. They can also be frozen for as long as 6 months. To defrost the frozen cakes, place them in the refrigerator for 24 hours before reheating.

Are you starting to think you may want to keep this Valentine around a little while longer? After he tastes your rich, decadent **chocolate molten cake,** his mind will be made up—then it's just up to you to make sure he's the right one.

BREAKING IT DOWN

I learned how to make a chocolate molten cake while working in one of my very first kitchen jobs. I was instructed to bake the cake in a super-hot oven for a short amount of time in order to create that gooey molten center. You might be able to get away with choosing a lower-quality chocolate if you're making something like buttercream frosting, but the quality of chocolate you use for this molten cake will determine the quality of the cake that comes out of the oven—so choose well! I recommend Valrhona chocolate, which you can find at many stores, including Trader Joe's.

You can make these cakes ahead of time and reheat them in the microwave or oven when you're ready to serve.

 # Chocolate Molten Cakes

INGREDIENTS	QUANTITY
Unsalted butter, warmed to room temperature	¾ stick (6 tablespoons)
Bittersweet chocolate	3 ounces
Egg yolks, warmed to room temperature	3 large
Whole eggs, warmed to room temperature	2 large
Confectioners' sugar	1 cup plus 4 tablespoons
Cake flour, sifted	⅓ cup plus 1 tablespoon

Preheat the oven to 400°F.

1. Melt the butter and chocolate together in a double boiler or in your microwave. See page 17 for details.

2. Combine the yolks and whole eggs together in a bowl (there's no need to whisk them together).

3. Add the butter–chocolate mixture to the bowl of a stand mixer fitted with the whisk attachment, or a mixing bowl (if using a hand mixer). Blend in the confectioners' sugar on low speed until smooth.

4. Continuing to operate the mixer on low speed, gradually add the egg mixture to the chocolate–sugar mixture until smooth.

5. Increase the mixer's speed to medium and add the sifted flour to the bowl all at once. Continue mixing until thoroughly blended.

6. Grease the ramekins (about 3" diameter) or cupcake pans with butter and then dust them with flour, or simply spray them with nonstick cooking spray.

7. Fill the ramekins with the batter until each is ¾ full.

8. Bake for 9 minutes at 400°F. The centers of the cakes will be very soft and gooey, so don't bother with the toothpick test.

9. Let the cakes sit for 3 to 4 minutes. If using a pan, invert to release the cakes. If using ramekins, place the hot ramekins on small plates for serving. Serve warm.

A Christmas dessert that will become a tradition

ACTIVE TIME 1½ hours

CHILL TIME

Prepare the pie crust dough (steps 1–6) the night before you plan to bake the pie so you can refrigerate it overnight.

YIELD One 9-inch pie

PREP

Take your eggs and butter out of the refrigerator a couple of hours before you make the pie dough.

Make the dough the night before you plan to make the pie.

Make the filling at least 1 hour before you're ready to bake the pie, because it has to rest before baking.

Preheat the oven to 375°F.

INGREDIENT FINDER

You should be able to find all the ingredients easily at your local supermarket.

GRAB THESE

Sifter

Baking sheet

9-inch pie pan

Stand mixer fitted with paddle attachment or a hand mixer

Rolling pin

Marble slab (or just clean off the kitchen counter with water mixed with a few drops of bleach), for rolling out dough

Wire rack

SHELF LIFE AND STORAGE INSTRUCTIONS

The baked pie will stay fresh for about 3 days stored in the refrigerator.

Mistletoe and ornaments might pop into your head when you think about Christmas, but to me, nothing says Christmas more than a slice of **sour cherry pie**. No matter how much my family and I eat at our traditional Christmas Eve dinner, we always manage to fit in a slice of this addictive dessert. (In fact, some people—I'm not naming names here—manage to choke down two or three slices.)

The sweet crumble topping and tart filling are such an irresistible combination that there's almost never any leftover pie. But on the rare chance that there might be a slice or two left over at your house, well, it makes a nice breakfast treat, too!

BREAKING IT DOWN

Save yourself a lot of time and effort by using frozen cherries for this recipe. They're already pitted, always available, and don't even have to be defrosted.

The reason it is best to let the dough rest overnight before baking is that it shrinks less once baked. An hour in the refrigerator will suffice, or if you are in a rush, you can cheat and skip making the pie crust. Instead, buy a frozen store-bought crust—already made, rolled, and in the pan, saving you a lot of time. Besides, it's the filling and crumble topping that make this pie so special.

 # Sour Cherry Pie

INGREDIENTS	QUANTITY
For Pie Crust:	
Ice water	3 tablespoons
Granulated sugar	1 teaspoon
Salt	½ teaspoon
Unsalted butter, warmed to room temperature	1 stick (8 tablespoons)
Egg yolk, warmed to room temperature	1
All-purpose flour, sifted	1⅓ cups
For Pie Filling:	
Granulated sugar	¾ cup
Corn starch	3 tablespoons
Salt	Pinch (1/16 teaspoon)
Fresh sour cherries, pitted (frozen cherries are easier, because they're already pitted and you don't even have to defrost them)	3⅔ cups (20 ounces) fresh or 1 (16-ounce) bag, frozen
Almond extract	¼ teaspoon
For Crumble Topping:	
All-purpose flour, sifted	¾ cup
Unsalted butter	1½ sticks (12 tablespoons)
Light brown sugar	½ cup
Granulated sugar	½ cup
Walnuts or pecans, chopped	½ cup
Ground cinnamon	2 teaspoons
Salt	Pinch (1/16 teaspoon)

MAKE, ROLL, AND PREBAKE THE CRUST:

1. Combine the ice water, sugar, and salt for the pie crust and set aside.

2. In the bowl of a stand mixer fitted with the paddle attachment, or in a mixing bowl (if using a hand mixer), cream the butter for the pie crust.

3. As the mixer continues to run, add the egg yolk for the pie crust to the butter, mixing thoroughly.

4. Add ¼ of the sifted flour for the pie crust and the water–sugar mixture to the bowl. Continue to mix until combined.

5. Add in the remaining flour in three more batches, mixing until just combined.

6. Shape the dough into a disk and wrap it in plastic wrap. Refrigerate overnight.

7. Preheat the oven to 375°F.

8. Lightly flour your work surface. Using a rolling pin, roll the dough into a disk with a ½-inch thickness.

9. Lift the dough over the pie pan and place it inside, pressing firmly on the center and sides to mold the dough to the pan. Using your index finger and thumb, pinch off any excess dough from the sides.

10. Prick the bottom of the dough with a fork. Place a piece of parchment paper over the dough and fill the lined pan with uncooked rice or pie weights to eliminate the possibility of the crust's puffing up while baking. Half-bake the pie crust at 375°F for about 15 minutes.

11. Remove the parchment paper and rice and let the crust cool completely, still inside the pan, on a wire rack (should be about 30 minutes).

MAKE THE FILLING AND CRUMBLE TOPPING:

1. Stir together the sugar, corn starch, and salt for the pie filling. Mix thoroughly.

2. Stir in the cherries and almond extract. Set the mixture aside for at least 1 hour.

3. In a medium bowl, combine all the ingredients for the crumble topping and stir until the mixture is combined and lumpy. Do not overmix.

ASSEMBLE AND BAKE THE PIE:

1. Stir the filling mixture well and pour it into the half-baked pie crust.

2. Sprinkle the crumble topping mixture on the pie and place the pie on a baking sheet.

3. Bake the pie at 375°F for 50 minutes, or until the top is golden brown and the filling is thick and bubbling. Remove from oven, cover with a sheet of foil,* and bake for another 15 minutes. Cool completely on a wire rack.

*Make sure the foil is punctured to ventilate the pie.

A soft, dreamy complement to your Easter brunch

ACTIVE TIME
1½ hours if you are not making the jam or 2 hours if you are making the jam

PROOF TIME
Two 1-hour proofs (for a total of 2 hours of proofing time)

YIELD
10–12 brioche

PREP
Take your eggs and butter out of the refrigerator a couple of hours before you make the brioche.

Preheat the oven to 375°F.

Grease the cupcake pans

Prepare the fresh compressed bakers' yeast (see page 26 for instructions).

Prepare the Raspberry Pepin jam recipe (see page 107).

INGREDIENT FINDER
You can usually purchase fresh compressed bakers' yeast at the bakery department of a fine supermarket. Just ask one of the people who works in the department. See page 26 for a discussion of the different types of yeast and the handling instructions for fresh compressed bakers' yeast. You can always substitute dry yeast instead (see the conversion in the ingredient list).

If you don't have heavy whipping cream on hand, you can substitute whole milk for the egg wash.

GRAB THESE
Candy thermometer

Stand mixer fitted with the dough hook attachment or a hand mixer

Greased cupcake pans

Candy thermometer

Rolling pin

Marble slab (or just clean off the kitchen counter with water mixed with a few drops of bleach), for rolling out dough

Pastry brush

Sifter

Raspberry Pepin Jam (see recipe on page 107)

Small offset spatula

Cutting board

Wire rack

SHELF LIFE AND STORAGE INSTRUCTIONS
1 day stored at room temperature.

Sick and tired of downing marshmallow peeps and chocolate bunnies from sunrise to sundown on Easter Sunday? This **chocolate–raspberry brioche** will give you the endurance you need to hunt for Easter eggs all day long. The homemade raspberry jam that oozes from its center is a delicious way to get your fruit for the day, and the bittersweet chocolate will jump-start your Easter sugar buzz.

BREAKING IT DOWN

Brioche is similar in taste to a croissant, but it is less flaky.

It's best to let the bread cool on a wire rack so it cools evenly.

My recipe tester and coworker Annie Smallwood passes along this great tip for proofing dough at home—put it in the microwave or even the dishwasher to sit while proofing so you maintain a nice warm temperature. Just be sure you don't turn either of those appliances on!

Brioche is best when eaten the day it's baked. However, if you have a few left over the next day, I recommend reheating them in the oven, toaster oven, or microwave if you are in a hurry.

Dusting your brioche with some confectioners' sugar, as shown in the photo on page 119, adds a more professional look and an extra hint of sweetness. Don't dust the brioche until they have cooled completely; otherwise, the sugar will just be absorbed into the brioche.

Be warned: This recipe requires a lot of patience and is for a more advanced baker, but the results are so worth it!

STEPHEN HAMILTON

🍵 Chocolate–Raspberry Brioche

INGREDIENTS	QUANTITY
For Brioche:	
Warm water (90°F)	3 tablespoons
Fresh compressed bakers' yeast (sold in square cakes)	1 cake (roughly 0.6 ounces) (you can also use 1 (2¼ teaspoon) "packet dry yeast"
All-purpose flour, sifted	⅓ cup
Sea salt	1½ teaspoons
Granulated sugar	⅛ cup
Bread flour	2½ cups
Whole eggs, warmed to room temperature	4 large
Unsalted butter, warmed to room temperature	2½ sticks (20 tablespoons, divided)
Raspberry Pepin Jam (see page 107)	1 cup
Miniature chocolate chips	1 cup
For Egg Wash:	
Whole eggs, warmed to room temperature	4 large
Heavy whipping cream	Dash
Sea salt	½ teaspoon

1. In the bowl of a stand mixer fitted with the dough hook attachment, or in a mixing bowl (if using a hand mixer), mix together the water and yeast and cover with the all-purpose flour. This mixture is called *poolish*. Let the poolish ferment for 20 minutes, until cracks form on the surface of the flour. Do not disturb the poolish as it ferments.

2. Add the salt, sugar, bread flour, and eggs to the poolish. Mix on high speed until the dough is very elastic and wraps around the hook, about 10 to 15 minutes.

3. Reduce the mixer speed to low and add half the butter. Mix until incorporated, about 2 to 3 minutes.

4. Increase the mixer speed to medium and add the remaining butter. Mix until incorporated, about 4 to 5 minutes. About halfway through the mix time, scrape the sides of the bowl all the way down to the bottom.

5. Remove the bowl from the mixer and allow the dough to rest and rise in a warm (around 75°F) place until it has doubled in volume, about 1 hour. This is called *proofing*. You can check to see if the dough has proofed enough by pressing lightly on it with your finger. The dough should be soft and should slowly spring back. If the dough still feels tough and quickly springs back, the dough has not proofed long enough. If your finger leaves a hole in the dough and doesn't spring back, the dough is overproofed.

6. Punch down the dough until it does not deflate any further. Cover and refrigerate for 1½ hours.

7. Punch down the dough again until it does not deflate any further. Cover and refrigerate overnight.

8. Prepare the egg wash by mixing together the eggs, heavy whipping cream, and salt by hand in a medium mixing bowl. Store in the refrigerator.

HOW TO SHAPE YOUR BRIOCHE

Preheat the oven to 375°F.

1. Remove the dough from the refrigerator. It is critical to work quickly so the dough does not become too warm.

2. Lightly flour your work surface, but be sure not to use too much flour. If you do, the dough won't stick to the table and form a tight seal.

3. Form the dough into a log. Using a rolling pin, roll the dough into a ½-inch-thick rectangle (about 18 × 10 inches).

4. Using a small offset spatula, spread a layer of the Raspberry Pepin Jam onto the brioche dough that covers all of the rectangle except the edges.

5. Sprinkle a layer of the miniature chocolate chips over the jam.

6. Roll the flattened dough with the jam and chips into a log, starting with the side farthest away from your body and rolling it toward your body. At the end of the rolling process, the point where the roll ends should face down onto the work surface and form a tight seal. Remove the log from the countertop and refrigerate it for 1 hour.

7. Slice the log into ten to twelve 1½-inch brioche pieces.

8. Place the brioche pieces into greased cupcake pans.

9. With a pastry brush, apply the egg wash to the tops of the brioche pieces.

10. Set the cupcake pans containing the brioche pieces aside and allow the brioche to proof until each piece doubles in volume, about 1 hour.

11. Bake at 375°F for 20 to 25 minutes, or until lightly browned. Cool completely on a wire rack.

Make everyone popovers worth waking up to ...

ACTIVE TIME 20 minutes

YIELD 10 popovers

PREP

Take your eggs and butter out of the refrigerator a couple of hours before you make the popovers.

Preheat oven to 375°F.

Spray muffin pans with cooking spray.

INGREDIENT FINDER

You can find everything at your local supermarket.

GRAB THESE

Muffin/cupcake pan

Mixing bowl

Whisk

Sifter

SHELF LIFE AND STORAGE INSTRUCTIONS

Best when eaten moments after they come out of the oven, but you can store them at room temperature for 1 to 2 days.

My uncle Page is known more as my family's in-house technical support guy, but it turns out that he has a few culinary tricks up his sleeve. I was first introduced to this recipe when my family and I vacationed in Keystone, Colorado, and Uncle Page came down from Denver to hang out. Uncle Page stumbled upon this wonderful **popovers** recipe while working as a cook on a barge en route to Baton Rouge, Louisiana.

This recipe is as easy as pie (don't worry, it's much easier than the **sour cherry pie** recipe!) and will truly impress your family when they're starving the morning after a big holiday dinner. You know you have to make something, but after slaving away in the kitchen preparing the family feast the day before, you want something super easy!

BREAKING IT DOWN

I love eating these popovers straight out of the oven with butter and jam, but you can easily spice up this recipe by adding cheese to the layers while pouring the batter into the cupcake pan. If you want to make this recipe sweet, add a ¼ cup of sugar to the melted butter.

 # Uncle Page's Popovers

INGREDIENTS	QUANTITY
Unsalted butter, melted	1 tablespoon
Milk, whole	1 cup
All-purpose flour, sifted	1 cup
Salt	¼ teaspoon
Whole eggs	3 large

Preheat the oven to 375°F.

1. In a small saucepan, melt the butter.

2. In a medium mixing bowl, combine the milk, butter, flour, and salt using a whisk. Mix until just combined.

3. In a small mixing bowl, whisk together the eggs.

4. Blend the eggs into the milk–butter mixture with a whisk until combined (the mixture will have the consistency of pancake batter).

5. Bake for 12 minutes at 375°F. Then reduce the oven temperature to 350°F and bake for another 6 to 8 minutes, or until golden brown.

ANNA BLESSING

Acknowledgments

I honestly feel a little embarrassed that my name is the only one on the cover of this book, because *Sweetness* would not have been possible without the time, recipes, testing, support, and hard work of so many of my friends, family, and coworkers. I would like to thank each of the talented people who contributed recipes: Rafael Ornelas, Chefs Jacquy Pfeiffer and Sebastien Canonne from the French Pastry School, Terry Levy, Eadie Levy, Alexa and Craig Sindelar, and Amy Grescowle. (For more information about my wonderful recipe contributors, please see page 10 in the Introduction.)

I am also lucky to be a member of an extremely supportive, smart, loving, and brutally honest family. Thanks to each of you for all of your support—Mom (Terry Levy, again), Dad (Mark Levy), Hillary Levy, Laura Levy, Paul Levy, Liz Gantz (Sugar), Jake Gantz, Grandma Eadie, Grandmother (Ann Lohr), Graysen Sanchez, and Deming Gantz.

I also want to extend a big thank you to all of the wonderful people I work with every day at Sarah's Pastries & Candies. Your talent, work ethic, and attitude truly inspire me.

Thanks to the talented photographers whose pictures are in this book: Anna Blessing (some food styling by Kristin Jensen) and Stephen Hamilton (food styling by Carol Smoler).

Thank you to the friends and family who took the time to test recipes for *Sweetness*: Erin Slater, Laura DuFour, Lizzie Kaplan, Marc Smoler, Margot Marsh, Annie Smallwood, Alexa Sindelar, Liz Gantz, Terry Levy, Perrin Davis, Adrienne Wagner, Chelsey Heller, Marla Seibold, Rachel Claff, and Diana Slickman. Thanks to the chefs I look up to, the people who have inspired me and who know that the simplest things are always the best: Martha Stewart, Ina Garten, Rafael Ornelas, Jacquy Pfeiffer, John Kraus, and Sebastien Canonne.

Thank you to my publisher, Doug Seibold, my editor, Perrin Davis, and the entire team at Agate Publishing for helping me every step of the way and sharing my passion for food. And to David Tamarkin, for your talent and generosity with words.

About the Author

Sarah Levy founded Sarah's Pastries & Candies in March 2004 by making chocolate candies out of her mom's kitchen. After a year, she had built up a wholesale business that includes Whole Foods Markets in the Midwest and smaller gourmet grocery shops; today, her business includes two retail locations in Chicago. She has been featured on Chicago television's *190 North, 24-7 Chicago,* and *Eye on Chicago* and in such publications as *Better Homes and Gardens*, *Elegant Bride*, *Complete Woman Magazine*, *Chicago Tribune*, *US Weekly*, *Chicago*, and *Time Out Chicago;* she has also been the dining editor for *Today's Chicago Woman* since April 2005. Sarah trained at several of the country's top restaurants and bakeries, including Spago Beverly Hills (where she apprenticed under James Beard Award–winning pastry chef Sherry Yard) and is a graduate of Northwestern University and the French Pastry School of Chicago.

ABOUT SARAH'S PASTRIES & CANDIES

Sarah's Pastries & Candies, which offers patrons consistently outrageously delicious pastries and chocolates, currently has two Chicago locations: one at 70 East Oak Street, in the heart of Chicago's Gold Coast, and one inside the Macy's store on State Street. Sarah's Pastries & Candies offers a wide array of morning pastries, brownies, cookies, petit fours, and cakes, all made from scratch daily, in the shops. Sarah's also offers chocolate candies and custom wedding cakes. For more information, or to order some of Sarah's delicious chocolate candies online, visit www.sarahscandies.com.

Anna Blessing

Index

Page numbers in *italics* indicate photographs.

A

"Active time," in recipes, 17–18
All-purpose flour, 22–23
Almond flour, 23
Almonds
    Decadent Chocolate–Almond Toffee, *103*, 104–105
    Mom's Almond Moon Cookies, *38*, 39–40
Amazon, 28
Amy's Amazing Carrot Cupcakes, 55, *56*, 57
Amy's Awesome Cream Cheese Frosting, 58, *59*
Applesauce
    Naked Cupcakes, *78*, 79–80
Apricots
    Rafael's Coconut–Apricot Macaroons, *120*, 121

B

Baking powder, 23
Baking sheet, 19
Baking soda, 23
Banana–Chocolate Chip Pound Cake, *86*, 87–89

Bench scraper, 19
Beverage, Green Goddess, 66
Bittersweet chocolate
    about, 24
    Banana–Chocolate Chip Pound Cake, *86*, 87–89
    Bittersweet Chocolate Chip Cookies, 99, *100*, 101
    Chocolate Molten Cakes, 122–123
    Decadent Chocolate–Almond Toffee, *103*, 104–105
    Vanilla Bean Chocolate Truffles, 111, *112*, 113
Black-and-White Cupcake Batter, *72*, 73–74
Brioche, Chocolate–Raspberry, 128, *129*, 130–131
Brownies
    Mom's Fudge Brownie Sundae, 69, *70*, 71
    Rafael's Righteous Cream Cheese Brownies, 41–42, *43*
Brown sugar, 26
Butter
    nut, 27
    unsalted, 26

C

Cakes
    Banana–Chocolate Chip Pound Cake, *86*, 87–89

Chocolate Molten Cakes, 112–123
Grandma Eadie's Double Chocolate
　　Chip Cake, 44
Carrots
　　Amy's Amazing Carrot Cupcakes, 55, *56*,
　　　57
Chef's knife, 22
Cherries
　　Sour Cherry Pie, *124*, 125–127
Chinois, 19
Chocolate
　　kinds of, 23–24
　　melting of, 17
　　tempering of, 18, 53
　　see also specific kinds
Chocolate chips
　　Chocolate–Raspberry Brioche, 128, *129*,
　　　130–131
　　Grandma Eadie's Double Chocolate
　　　Chip Cake, 44
Chocolate pistoles, 24
Cocoa butter, 23
Cocoa paste/cocoa liquor/cocoa mass, 24
Cocoa powder
　　about, 23–24
　　Fantastically Fudgy Vanilla and Cocoa
　　　Icing, 75–76, *77*
　　Naked Cupcakes, *78*, 79–80
　　Sinful Chocolate Soufflés, 81–83
　　Supreme Chocolate Cupcakes, *60*,
　　　61–62
　　Vanilla Bean Chocolate Truffles, 111,
　　　112, 113
Coconut
　　Rafael's Coconut–Apricot Macaroons,
　　　120, 121
Confectioners' sugar, 26

Cookies
　　about, decorating of, 49
　　Bittersweet Chocolate Chip Cookies,
　　　99, *100*, 101
　　Holiday Vanilla Bean Sugar Cookies,
　　　45, *46*, 47
　　Lemon Baby Rattle Cookies, 114, *115*,
　　　116
　　Mom's Almond Moon Cookies, 38,
　　　39–40
　　Rafael's Toffee Sugar Cookies, 108,
　　　109, 110
Corn syrup, 26
Couverture chocolate, 24
Cream cheese
　　Amy's Awesome Cream Cheese Frosting,
　　　58, *59*
　　Rafael's Righteous Cream Cheese
　　　Brownies, 41–42, *43*
Creaming, 17
Cream of tartar, 23
Cucumber
　　Green Goddess, 66
Cupcakes
　　about, frosting of, 65
　　Amy's Amazing Carrot Cupcakes, 55,
　　　56, 57
　　Black-and-White Cupcake Batter, *72*,
　　　73–74
　　Naked Cupcakes, *78*, 79–80
　　Supreme Chocolate Cupcakes, *60*,
　　　61–62

D

Dark chocolate
　　about, 24

Dark chocolate (continued)
 Chocolate Buttercream Frosting, *63*,
  64–65
 Decadent Chocolate-Covered
  Strawberries, *51*, *52*, 53–54
Decadent Chocolate–Almond Toffee,
 103, 104–105
Decadent Chocolate-Covered
 Strawberries, *51*, *52*, 53–54
Decorating materials, 24, 26
Demarle, 28
Difficulty rating symbol, 9
Digital kitchen scale, 19
Double boiler, melting chocolate in, 17
Dough, proofing of, 128, 131

E

Eggs
 tempering of, 18
 using large, 26
Equipment, 18–22, 27–28
 in recipe chart, 31–33

F

Fantastically Fudgy Vanilla and Cocoa
 Icing, 75–76, *77*
Feuilletine, 27
Filling, Pistachio Buttercream, 96, *97*, 98
Flavorants, 27
Flours, 22–23
Fondant, 24, 26
Food processor, 22
French Pistachio Macarons, 92, *93*, 94–95

Frosting/icing
 Amy's Awesome Cream Cheese
  Frosting, 58, *59*
 Chocolate Buttercream Frosting, *63*,
  64–65
 Fantastically Fudgy Vanilla and Cocoa
  Icing, 75–76, *77*
 Royal Icing, 48–49

G

Glucose syrup, 26
Grandma Eadie's Double Chocolate Chip
 Cake, 44
Granola, *85*, 90–91
Granulated sugar, 26
Grapes
 Green Goddess, 66
Green Goddess, 66
Gum paste, 24

H

Hand grater, 19
Hand mixer, 22
Holiday Vanilla Bean Sugar Cookies, 45,
 46, 47
Honey
 Mom's Granola, *85*, 90–91

I

Ice cream/cookie scoop, 20–21
Icing. *See* Frosting/icing

Ingredients
    chocolate, 23–24
    decorating materials, 24, 26
    dry, 22–23
    flavorants, 27
    general, 26–27
    recipe chart, 30–31
    shopping for, 27
    weight of, 18, 28 29

J

Jam, Raspberry Pepin, *106*, 107
JB Prince, 27

K

Kerekeds, 27
King Arthur Flour, 28
Kitchen scale, 19
Knives, 22
Kosher salt, 23

L

Lecithin, 24
Lemon Baby Rattle Cookies, 114, *115*, 116
Loaf pan, 18

M

Macarons, French Pistachio, 92, *93*, 94–95

Macaroons, Rafael's Coconut–Apricot, *120*, 121
Mascarpone cheese
    Banana–Chocolate Chip Pound Cake, *86*, 87–89
Measuring cups, 19–20
Melting technique, 17
Metal offset spatula, 20
Methods and techniques, 17–18
Microplane hand grater, 19
Microwave, melting chocolate in, 17
Milk, tempering of, 18
Milk chocolate
    about, 24
    Vanilla Bean Chocolate Truffles, 111, *112*, 113
Mixers, 22
Mixing bowls, 19
Mom's Almond Moon Cookies, *38*, 39–40
Mom's Fudge Brownie Sundae, 69, *70*, 71
Mom's Granola, *85*, 90–91

N

Naked Cupcakes, *78*, 79–80
Nut butter, 27

O

Oats
    Mom's Granola, *85*, 90–91

P

Paring knife, 22

Pastry bags, 20
Pastry brush, 20
Pastry Chef Central, 27, 28
Pecans
    Amy's Amazing Carrot Cupcakes, 55,
        56, 57
    Bittersweet Chocolate Chip Cookies,
        99, *100*, 101
Pie, Sour Cherry, *124*, 125–127
Pistachio Buttercream Filling, Rafael's,
    96, *97*, 98
Popovers, Uncle Page's, 132
Praline paste, 27
Proofing, of dough, 128, 131

R

Rafael's
    Coconut–Apricot Macaroons, 120, *121*
    Pistachio Buttercream Filling, 96, *97*, 98
    Righteous Cream Cheese Brownies,
        41–42, *43*
    Toffee Sugar Cookies, 108, *109*, 110
Raisins
    Mom's Granola, *85*, 90–91
Ramekins, 18
Raspberries
    Chocolate–Raspberry Brioche, 128,
        129, 130–131
    Naked Cupcakes, *78*, 79–80
    Raspberry Pepin Jam, *106*, 107
Rolling pins, 20
Royal Icing, 48–49
Rubber spatula, 20

S

Salts, 23
Scale, 19
Scoops, 20–21
Sea salt, 23
Semisweet chocolate, 24
Serrated knife, 22
Sheet tray, 19
Sieve, 22
Sifter, 22
Sifting, 18
Silpat sheets, 18–19, 28
Sinful Chocolate Soufflés, 81–83
Soufflés, Chocolate, Sinful, 81–83
Sour Cherry Pie, *124*, 125–127
Spatulas, 20
Stand mixer, 22
St. Germain liqueur
    Green Goddess, 66
Strainer, 22
Strawberries
    Decadent Chocolate-Covered
        Strawberries, *51*, *52*, 53–54
Sugars, 26
Sundae, Mom's Fudge Brownie, *69*, *70*, 71
Supreme Chocolate Cupcakes, *60*, 61–62

T

Table salt, 23
Tart ring, 19
Tempering, 18, 53
Tequila
    Green Goddess, 66
Thermometer, 19
Timer, 19

Toffee, Decadent Chocolate–Almond, *103*, 104–105
Truffles, Vanilla Bean Chocolate, 111, *1 12*, 113

U

Uncle Page's Popovers, 132
Unsalted butter, 26
Unsweetened chocolate
    about, 24
    Mom's Fudge Brownie Sundae, *69*, *70*, 71
    Rafael's Righteous Cream Cheese Brownies, 41–42, *43*

V

Vanilla beans
    Holiday Vanilla Bean Sugar Cookies, *45*, *46*, 47
    Lemon Baby Rattle Cookies, 114, *115*, 116
    Sinful Chocolate Soufflés, 81–83
    Vanilla Bean Chocolate Truffles, 111, *112*, 113
Vanilla extract, 27
Vanilla paste, 27

W

Walnuts
    Mom's Fudge Brownie Sundae, *69*, *70*, 71
Weight, of ingredients, 18, 28–29

Wheat germ
    about, 23
    Mom's Granola, *85*, 90–91
Whisks, 20
White chocolate
    about, 24
    Decadent Chocolate-Covered Strawberries, *51*, *52*, 53–54
Wilton, 27–28
Wire rack, 18

Y

Yeast, 26–27